No Bad Dates

The Dating Advice You Actually Need

Kari Tumminia

Copyright © 2020 Kari Tumminia
All rights reserved.
ISBN: 978-0-578-64670-1

DEDICATION

To the great spiritual teachers, healers, and mentors that have supported me along my journey to wholeness. To every person I've dated before, may you each find the happiness you deserve, and nothing less. And, most importantly, to my endlessly supportive, astoundingly handsome husband, without whom I would not have the space or availability to indulge in great endeavors like this.

And, of course, to you. May you find comfort, healing, inspiration, and laughter in the pages of this book.

CONTENTS

	Introduction	1
1	There are No Accidents	9
2	Consciousness is King	16
3	Always Opt for Authentic	40
4	Boundaries, Boundaries, Boundaries	56
5	Get Clear About Alignment	80
6	Expansion or Nothing	104
7	It's All Icing on the Cake, Baby	129
8	Leave the Past Where It Belongs	147
9	Feel Your Way	168
10	Learn Your Love Substitutes Non-Negotiable	191
11	Tight Pants Aren't Always the Answer	218
12	You Deserve Magic	240
13	The Two Requirements	254
14	Self Love is Non-Negotiable	264
15	There Are No Bad Dates	279

– INTRODUCTION –

Hello, love! I am so glad you're here.

First things first: If you're ready to have an amazing, fulfilling love life and you're willing to show up and do the deep work, you absolutely, 100% can– and WILL. It doesn't matter what kind of relationship your parents had, or how many bad dates you've been on, or how gut-wrenchingly horrible your last relationship was. You deserve love. You ARE love. And all of the love you can possibly handle is already out there, waiting for you to align with it and allow it into your life, in whatever way you want it to show up.

Don't worry if you haven't figured it out yet– I'm assuming that's why you're here in the first place. There's nothing wrong with you if you've struggled, have trouble believing that any of this is really, truly possible, or if you aren't married with 2.5 kids and a house in the suburbs by age 30. Love is one of the most talked about topics out there, and it is *loaded* with stuff that isn't always serving our best and highest potential. We want a relationship, yet we want to be independent; we want to be wanted, yet we resent it when potential partners come on too strong; we work so damn hard not to appear too needy/emotional/undesirable, yet we want someone to accept us for who we are. Not to mention, it can seem like everyone has a hand in our relationship stuff– mom and dad, childhood beliefs, old flames, the latest magazine-stand advice on how to get and keep the guy you want, the entire internet, and even that estranged aunt you only see at weddings and funerals who always wants to know why you're not married yet.

Love can be confusing and overwhelming, and the truth is, most of us spend our lives approaching it in a way that makes us a victim and removes our power. The good news is, you're not alone. With the right tools and guidance and a few perspective shifts for good measure, you can learn to approach love, dating, and relationships from an entirely new place full of power, fulfillment, and joy. You're already starting this profound transformation by showing up right here. All you need to do is release what's limiting you, make new, intentional choices about where you're headed next, how you get there, and who you get there with, get wise about yourself and your deepest desires, and put yourself out there in new, exciting ways.

I personally transformed my love story in a way that was so profound and so dramatically fast that the people who know me best still haven't quite figured out what happened, or how. I was the queen of dysfunctional relationships fueled by resentment over my past and a bad habit of making self-destructive relationship choices. So many times in my life, it seemed like I had everything else going for me, but I just couldn't figure out love.

Somewhere in my mid-twenties, just when I thought I'd be married, looking at houses, and maybe even thinking about china patterns and kids, I found myself suddenly un-engaged (just two months before my wedding, no less), head spinning, and wondering what went wrong. I had been sure that I was done with the process of dating, having to find a relationship, and figuring out how to fit together with someone else. Yet, there I was, standing in a nearly-empty bedroom of a house that didn't have the chance to feel like my own, waiting for the guy I was supposed to marry to come pick up his stuff and begin the process of untangling. When he got there, I broke down into tears. I begged him to stay. I made all sorts of promises, plans, and offered up countless ways I would be better, different, or make things easier. Part of me expected him to stay– we were *engaged* after all. Invitations had been addressed. We had a venue and a caterer. I had a wedding dress.

Another part of me expected him to follow through with leaving– deep down I knew that things hadn't felt great recently. This part of me thought maybe he would cry a little, tell me it was him and not me, and leave with enough remorse and sadness to match the tears I had been crying for days. And, honestly, maybe I was even hoping for a little breakup sex to symbolize just how difficult is was to walk away for good. What I did not expect was for him to stop at the door, turn, walk over to me as I sat on the bed, look deep into my eyes, and say, "Look, I just don't love you that way. I'm not sure I ever did," and walk out without so much as a wave.

Hindsight, as they say, is 20/20, and it's a hell of a lot easier to tell that story now than it was then. Right this moment, while writing these paragraphs to you, I am sitting in a fancy Japanese restaurant waiting for my husband to arrive and have dinner with me. I already know without question that we'll have an amazing time with lots of laughter and conversation, after which we'll head back to our house in the middle of the woods, sit out on the deck and enjoy coffee and the weather. There will be no shortage of things to talk about, laugh about, and smile about. We'll head to bed when I get tired and we'll have amazing sex, because our connection is just that good, and he'll hold me until we both fall asleep. I don't say all that to brag to you about my life, or to make things sound like an impossible fairy tale, or even to sell more books – I say all that to illustrate contrast. I can practically map the course of our evening because I know my relationship– and I know my relationship because long before I met my husband, I got clear around what I was looking for. I learned to understand myself (and what worked for me) on an intimate level, I got rid of the old stories that used to dictate my dysfunctional dating patterns, and I manifested a real relationship that really worked.

And you can too.

Before we dive in, we have to get a few things straight right off the bat:

1. I am not your fairy godmother. So if you're expecting this book to turn pumpkins into carriages and give you permission to run around in the middle of the night losing shoes in the name of finding love, you'll have to take your expectations elsewhere. The same goes for staying in dysfunctional relationships, chasing unavailable partners (no matter how much you're sure they must be your soul mate), and sacrificing your authenticity or well being to avoid being

alone. This book isn't designed to tell you what you want to hear, it's designed to tell you what you need to know.

2. There is no Prince or Princess Charming, and this book will not bring you any closer to finding him. If you want to be regaled with stories of the one, single person that was created specifically for you, will effortlessly fulfill all of your wildest dreams, and make you endlessly happy, this isn't the book for you. We'll talk more about Prince Charming later on, but it probably won't be in the way you'd expect from a book about dating and love. Love is available to you in an infinite number of forms and it can come in a wide variety of packages that are all worthy and can all be genuinely, truly good. There is no magic needle in the haystack that you have to find before you can be happy.

3. I can't make the promise that you'll never have another unsatisfactory date again– I have yet to figure out how to influence the entire population of available persons in the

dating pool (but when I do, I will *absolutely* let you know!)– and in the process of finding that healthy, aligned relationship you've been looking for, you just might have to sort through a few who don't align with you– but I can promise that after reading this book you'll have gained the ability to look at those less-than-stellar dates from a whole new perspective. You'll be able to see the red flags coming a lot sooner. And even better, you just might find yourself naturally attracting a higher caliber of potential candidates.

If you want to let go and finally be done with the love lessons from your parents, your past, and even whatever you may have picked up from the latest issue of your guilty-pleasure magazine– because, let's be honest, if those worked, you probably wouldn't be reading this book right now– we can do that together.

If you're looking for a new way to approach dating and love that's unquestionably empowering, this book is for you.

If you're ready to finally show up for yourself and unapologetically pursue life and love in a way that reflects your unquestionable worth and your unique amazingness – welcome! You're in the right place.

– CHAPTER ONE –
THERE ARE NO ACCIDENTS

The most obvious place to start in any love story is at the beginning. The path that brought you to this point and to this book is yours and yours alone. There is no way for me to know what your love and dating experiences have involved up until this point, but I do know that whatever you've been through and whatever your past holds, it does not define you. It definitely does not define the potential of your future love-life. When I was planning this book, I began to imagine the place I had been in when I started to heal my relationship patterns. It was a mental space I've seen reflected in so many of my clients over the years– feeling a little bit frustrated, discouraged, alone, and like something might be wrong with them because they hadn't been able to solve the relationship puzzle like so many of their friends, family members, and peers seemingly had. So, the first step I want to help you make in your own personal love revolution is one of grace and hope.

Your personal love story, as it stands so far, holds meaning, but it doesn't mean anything about you. Let me explain– your past relationships, crushes, divorces, breakups, bad dates, frustrations, patterns, and so on, hold insight, lessons, and information that you can use to evolve and grow. At the same time, all of those experiences are not intended to limit or define you– or your love life– in any way. Your future isn't dependent on your past, but in order to stop repeating all that old-relationship stuff and separate your future potential from everything that's already been, you have to recognize that something different is even possible in the first place. For many of us, that can be incredibly difficult. Afterall, we only know what we know and our minds work on evidence.

Equally as important– no matter what your past relationships have brought your way, I can assure you that there isn't anything wrong with you. You are not broken.

I'll say it again for those in the back– **YOU ARE NOT BROKEN.**

It doesn't matter how many bad dates you've had. It doesn't matter how many failed relationships you have under your belt. And it definitely doesn't matter how old you are. Whatever brought you to this moment and this book, you are exactly where you are meant to be. Consider this your invitation to more– you can change everything about your love life starting at this very moment. The very next date you go on can be different. You have the power to change everything.

Wondering where to start? You already have! This book is filled with dating and relationship advice you actually need– no tactics, no fluff, no niceties. Just by opening this up and reading this very first chapter, you're already on your way to taking back the reins of your love life and making some massive mindset shifts that will empower you to see and do everything differently. For the time being, my story and the stories of my clients will be your evidence, and in no time at all, you'll be well on your way to creating new evidence of bigger and better things yourself.

Before you go any further, take a moment, right now, to give yourself credit for everything you've been through. Really, go ahead (chances are you probably don't do that enough). Acknowledge all of your effort, your heartache, and your frustration. Pat yourself on the back for sticking it out through that terrible date... or dates. Show yourself gratitude for surviving that break up. Appreciate yourself, even for all of the times that you've struggled. Even in the moments of deep pain. Even in the midst of the relationships that were oh-so-wrong, but that you tried to make work anyway. Even in the moments where you may have been in the wrong. Gratitude. Appreciation. Acknowledgement. Grace.

Trust me when I tell you that there is nothing to be gained by dwelling in the past or playing the blame game. You won't fix your love life or change the way you date by assigning fault or resigning yourself to spinster status because of how things have gone before. If you struggle with this, consider taking a test run on a new mantra: *"Even though things haven't always worked out the way I wanted them to, I was doing the best I could with what I knew. That was then, this is now."* (Bonus Tip: Repeat this mantra every day, out loud, in the mirror, and whenever you're feeling low about your relationship history).

I want to invite you to put some space between you and your past. Sure, acknowledge it for what it is, but I challenge you not to use it to create or apply meaning about yourself or the world– or all of the gorgeous, juicy, romantic potential hanging out in your future.

What you do need to pay attention to is the insight and purpose your storied relationship past holds. By that, I mean what you can learn and recognize about yourself through the lens of your past relationship experiences. Just like it is no accident that you're here, at this very moment, reading this book, the interactions you've had weren't by accident either. The second truth I'd like to invite you to consider is that each and every relationship you've had, from bad dates to long-term situations, holds great opportunities for you to learn and grow. Everything in the universe is working together to support your evolution and your expansion. You are here to learn and grow and love, and some of the best learning and growing moments happen in our relationships with others. There is nothing like the mirror of another person to really show us exactly what we need to learn about ourselves – and each of your specific relationships is no exception.

Even when it comes to your past, there are still no accidents. Your relationships were not happenstance or incidental. They were on purpose; specifically, *your* purpose. Let that sink in for just a moment. What would change in your life if you were able to embrace the idea that all of your past relationships contributed to the inner-workings of the person you're becoming? What if all of your bad dates, failed relationships, and exes were actually moving you along a path of evolution and expansion?

Whoa. Talk about a shift in perspective.

If that were true – and I do mean "if" – I would totally understand if you weren't quite there with me yet – but IF that were true, might it then be possible for you to find gratitude for all of your past relationships? Each and every one? And might it then be possible that you are exactly where you're meant to be in terms of your big-picture love life? And perhaps it's also possible to heal your heart and do the soul-searching, perspective-shifting learning for yourself so that you can make energetic space to manifest epic love into your life?

Spoiler alert: It's totally possible.

And that, my friend, is exactly why you're here. Because there are no accidents. This moment is on purpose. And no matter where you're coming from, I'm here to assure you that you aren't broken, you're learning. You are not cursed in love, you're evolving. And all those love stories you've been living to, as if they were limitations? They're just propelling you forward into what's truly possible.

Throughout the following chapters, I'm going to introduce you to my Rules of Better Love– these mindset shifts are powerful passages that will lead you to approach your love life from a place of intention, purpose, and personal power. Each chapter will immerse you in one facet of dating to create better love and end with exercises to help you bring the perspective shifts home and apply them in your real life. These shifts in perspective and the real-life practices I give you work. I used them for myself, and I've used them with my coaching clients over the past decade. The more you commit to actually doing the exercises, challenging yourself to gain new insight and understanding, the more change will be possible. I cannot wait to hear your love story and witness your transformation!

– CHAPTER TWO –
CONSCIOUSNESS IS KING

If you're truly ready to be done with the bad dates and unsatisfactory relationships, you have to be willing to choose to be conscious in every encounter you have. One of the greatest challenges when it comes to creating new, healthy relationships is that we are so prone to falling into unconscious patterns when it comes to how we relate to others. Here's what happens– we are perpetually focused on the lack of partnership, intimacy, and love in our lives, and we begin to think that our ideal life is contingent on meeting the right person, being swept off our feet, and falling in love. Because we're so fairy tale, happily-ever-after, and prince/princess charming oriented, we miss the opportunity to be fully present in what's actually happening right now. In other words, most of us don't date to enjoy and learn from the process, we date because we're desperately trying to create something we believe to be missing from our lives. And because all of our energy is funneled into getting what we think we need and finding what we believe is missing, we cut corners in the process. And even worse, we forget to really live while we're at it.

Consider your favorite meal at your favorite restaurant. It probably represents foods, flavors, and an experience that you really enjoy. Chances are, you know, on some level, why you like that particular combination of foods. You may even repeat those preferences throughout other meals, even when you aren't in your all time favorite restaurant, and given the objective choice it probably isn't hard to pick that meal. Now imagine you were stranded on a desert island, starving. In this situation, food has become a source of insecurity— you know you need it and want it, but you don't know how or when you'll get it. Even though your food preferences didn't disappear the moment you ended up tragically stranded, and you would likely still have memory of that favorite meal at that favorite restaurant in this scenario, the selection of food you're willing to tolerate would become much broader. You may even eat things you couldn't imagine eating before your circumstances around food became more desperate. Your love life works much the same way. Desperation, insecurity, and a focus on what you believe you're lacking lowers your standards. If you live in a place where you believe love is what's missing and only another person can remedy that, you'll accept far less than what you deserve, sometimes without even realizing it.

    I get it. You want the perfect partner. You want to be done with dating. You imagined that you'd be married by age [fill in the blank] and you're frustrated that you seem no closer to your relationship goals than before. Focusing on the lack and desperately trying to fill the empty space means you're missing out on the process; and the process, darling, is the whole magical purpose of dating. Like crafting that elaborate, favorite meal, it requires engagement, attention, and faith that the steps required in the recipe will result in culinary perfection.

See, you don't get to skip chapters of your relationship book or steps in your relationship recipe. Every line, every character, every conflict, and every moment is preparing you for something bigger. Dating consciously, in part, means that you develop the ability to see your encounters from the perspective of something larger, some place higher with a clearer view and more understanding. Then, in that process, you make a conscious decision to take off your rose colored glasses. In other words, you choose to see things for what they actually are.

When we date unconsciously, we disengage from the process of meeting, getting to know, enjoying (or not), and choosing (or not) another person. In our checked-out state, we totally miss [read: ignore] red flags. We attach our expectations, our hopes, our dreams, and our fantasies to a person, often without their consent or actual participation. We make compromises, move too fast, avoid real connection, and explain-away the obvious signs that our partner is seriously not aligned with what we actually want or need. We use the sex and the rush of physical chemistry as a replacement for actual intimacy and compatibility. We end up eating cold pizza out of the garbage instead of savoring a five star meal.

    I always imagined that I would marry young. I was the type of girl that didn't date much as a teenager, and, thanks to one-too-many rom coms, I assumed that meant I would end up someone's diamond-in-the-rough and love would just magically find me. You know, like the girl in the movie who is awkward and loveless until the popular girl who took pity on her convinces her to take off her glasses and cut her hair, and then suddenly she's gorgeous and love strikes without warning? It may sound silly, but it was the story I told myself to compensate for the fact that I felt like something was wrong with me for not dating more, or when the dates I did go on fizzled and failed miserably.

    Several years into my twenties, I still wasn't any closer to being married than I had been at 18. While I had dated some, I was still waiting for the magic to happen. Part of me didn't understand what was taking so long, and another part of me felt so insecure in the dating process that I just wanted it to be over– I wanted to find my person, and stat. The problem was, I didn't want to find my person to add to my rich, amazing life experience, I wanted to find my person to be done with the process because the process felt painful and difficult.

It was that insecurity that often led me to move faster than I was really comfortable with in my relationships. I wanted to be chosen, but deep down, I believed I wasn't good enough in some way. To make up for it, I tried to take on the role of the girl who was down for anything. I believed that if I matched the pace of whomever I was with, I'd increase my chances of being loved, being accepted, and being picked. I was so focused on the goal of creating the happily-ever-after relationship I wanted that I put up with way more than I should have or needed to. I made exceptions, excuses, and created explanations for my partners when they were lacking in any way. I tried to become "the cool girl."

I was trying to create my ideal love life with a bunch of people who didn't actually fit the role. It was like working with a stunt double and trying to pretend they were the real-deal. And it would have been really obvious that my partners at the time were anything but the real thing, but every time my fantasy was threatened, I chose, on some level, not to see it.

When I met Scott, it was easy to make him fit into the idea of my ideal relationship as long as I ignored or explained away the red flags I insisted at the time were just minor details. See, Scott very much wanted his own end-goal relationship, and he made no effort to hide the fact that he wanted to get married, have kids, a dog, and a house in the suburbs, preferably with a white picket fence. He said all the right future-oriented things, and it was just enough to make me believe that I was finally on the right track.

Sure, he smoked and I hated it. Sure, he wore nothing but band t-shirts and ill-fitting jeans. But I liked that he was a musician and I filed it away as all a part of the front-man persona. I rationalized that when we settled down and had kids, he wouldn't need to do those things anymore. I told myself (and my friends) that I was totally okay with the misalignments because he was creative and sensitive. Sure, he asked me out via drunk text at 2am, but I had been out at the time too, so it was totally fine right? Sure, his family didn't like me, his dad refused to speak to me at all, and my sisters hated him, but our families weren't the ones in the relationship, right? And sure, he changed jobs more frequently than I changed my socks and never seemed to be able to make a serious commitment or a serious plan, didn't own a suit, and spent most of his time playing video games, talking about cars or skateboarding, but I could compensate for those things if I just showed him how much more was out there that he just hadn't experienced yet. And when he moved in without there ever being an official conversation about what was happening, and we had our first big fight about whether he should smoke in the apartment or not, I told myself it was all part of the process. And I had wanted a serious live-in boyfriend anyway, right?

One night before Christmas, about 6 months into our relationship, Scott proposed. We had gone out that night and saw a local band at a tiny dive bar. We drank. And as we fell into bed at 3am, completely intoxicated, he pulled out a ring box and set it on the bed. "Marry me," he said, looking at me expectantly.

I said yes. I told myself the nausea was from the alcohol and passed out.

The next morning, I woke in my sun-filled loft and immediately regretted my decision to drink so much the night before. In my hangover haze, I noticed the ring on my left hand and it all came flooding back. Thankfully, Scott had left for work early that morning and he wasn't there to witness my intense, panic-filled rant as I ran around the apartment remembering that I was betrothed.

    I asked my dog at least twenty times what on earth I had done.

    I asked my cat if I had lost my damn mind.

    I asked my houseplants what I was going to do and how I was going to do it before Scott got home from work.

    And, above all else, I did not call my mom, who would surely be criticizing and disappointed, or worse, actually excited and ask how he did it. Not wanting to explain to her that I didn't actually remember because of the sheer number of vodka cranberries I drank the night before, I did what any girl would do in a moment of sheer panic and fear that was entirely inappropriate to share with family– I called my best friend.

    He answered on the first ring. Before he had a chance to say anything, I blurted out, "I did something bad."

    "What happened? Are you okay?"

"Scott proposed. I said yes."

He insisted I come over immediately. I got dressed, tried to look slightly less hung-over, and made my way across the city to his University City apartment. I walked in without knocking and threw myself down on his futon as dramatically as one can on a piece of furniture that was situated so close to the ground. Hand draped over my eyes in fainting fashion, I lamented my predicament.

I was engaged. I agreed to be engaged while I was wildly intoxicated. I was engaged to a guy I was not sure I wanted to marry. Hell, whether or not I wanted to live with him fluctuated from week to week. We had been dating for six months and I had been overlooking and ignoring and bargaining away all of the things I couldn't stand about him, all of the red flags, and now I was suddenly promised to be married, of all things.

John had been my best friend since junior high. He looked at me with all of the calm wisdom any twenty-something who hadn't just promised themselves in marriage to a terrible match could muster and said, "You're engaged... to Scott. I'm not one hundred percent sure why, or what you're going to do about it, but just breathe.

Because you aren't married, you're just engaged. I'm making you oatmeal."

He did, in fact, make me oatmeal. And I ate it. And it did make me feel better in a strange, taken-care-of kind of way. He then suggested I take off my new engagement ring and stay at his place for the rest of the day until I was more ready to deal with things. His family was visiting and it would be a good distraction.

I hid my engagement ring in my John's silverware drawer while I spent time with his family and pretended nothing had happened for the next thirteen hours. I avoided my phone, any and all questions about my relationship, and tried not to think about any of it. It would end up taking me two weeks of rationalizing, pros and cons lists, and inner conflict before I decided what to do about my engagement.

And if you guessed that I maturely and gently broke it off while returning the ring because I knew in my gut it wasn't right, and because no girl wants to stay in the engagement that caused her to hide in someone else's apartment for nearly an entire weekend… you'd be wrong. My insecurities and unconscious fears and beliefs kicked into hyper drive that weekend. I rationalized that he wouldn't have proposed if he didn't really love me and I could fix everything else. I told myself that love was what really mattered and all the things I was unhappy about were just details.

You might be thinking that this is a pretty cut and dry example of something you would never do– ya know, accept a drunk proposal, immediately regret it, hide your engagement ring, disappear for a weekend and end up staying engaged to the guy anyway– and I'd probably agree with you. I sincerely hope there are not that many women out there who were so deeply troubled by their own engagement that they responded the way I did, but I'd bet my britches that you've done exactly the same thing on a smaller scale.

True, I unconsciously dated my way into an equally unconscious engagement. And I totally ignored the giant red flags along the way. And I kept ignoring them when I stayed with the guy for another two years (yeah, you read that right), but how many times have you ignored a giant red flag, or two, in the name of making it work? How many times have you known, in your gut, that a guy was just wrong for you, but you stuck it out in the name of seeing what would come of it or giving it a fair chance? How many times have you overlooked, ignored, or explained away major misalignments in a relationship because your fear of being alone or being rejected was bigger than your commitment to finding a person who's truly right for you? Or how many times have you settled for less because you truly believed that you could save or fix or love that person into being better?

    I wasn't honest with myself or my partner in my relationship with Scott– not when we were dating and not when we were engaged. I knew in my gut that we weren't a good match, and I started out in our relationship wanting to change him to make it work. I rationalized that the details of our day-to-day interactions would be overshadowed by love, but the truth is, in my quest to settle down and be done with dating, I convinced myself I could make a relationship work that was doomed from the start. I attached my fantasies and my desires to a person who could never have fulfilled them because he genuinely wasn't right for me. It wasn't that he was wrong in and of himself, or that he was less-than in any way, but by ignoring my gut, ignoring the red flags, and explaining away everything that seemed like it didn't fit, I was actually playing a role in keeping both of us from finding partners who were more well-suited to who we were.

I had chosen to see what I wanted to see and not what was really there. I was focused on the potential future I thought I could create with the person I was with and not the actual person I was with. I wasn't present in my relationship.

Conscious dating is challenging on a number of levels, but I find that most people struggle to commit to take responsibility for their own role in all of their relationships, and to stop the bad, unconscious habit of dating another person's potential. One of my favorite dating questions to ask my clients is this: "If you look at the person you're with and remove all of the future plans, all of the promises, all of the fantasies about how things could be or will be eventually, all of the potential of the person you know they could one day be, and nothing changed from this point forward, would you still want to be with them?"

It isn't that people can't or don't change, grow, or evolve, it's that there's no guarantee how or when any person will. If we're seeing people for who they really are (no rose colored glasses, remember?), and we're seeing our own patterns and roles in our relationships, we can't date someone's potential, because potential isn't reality. This lesson is sometimes really obvious, like when a girl is dating a guy who's married and he promises over and over again that he's going to leave his wife. You and I both know how that story usually ends— she waits and sacrifices her own needs and wellbeing and he never actually leaves his wife. But other times, it isn't so straightforward, as I helped my client Morgan see.

Morgan had been dating a guy for just over a year. They got along well, lived in the same city, and spent time together each week that they both seemed to genuinely enjoy. Morgan assured me that she had no complaints about her boyfriend— he was great and she thought they were well matched. But, she hated his friends.

At the time, her boyfriend was living in a large house with a group of guys he had gone to college with. It had an unmistakable frat-house vibe and all the guys threw parties every weekend to unwind from the work week. Morgan's boyfriend in particular worked what she described as a very high-pressure, demanding job in finance; he was very successful and had big plans for their future, something he talked about with her often. All of the plans he made hinged on his eventual success at the firm he worked for, which made Morgan very prone to making exceptions for any poor behavior linked to his work. When he missed dinner plans or canceled dates last minute, it was often because of work. When he partied on the weekends, it was because his job was so stressful that he needed an outlet. When she brought up things she was unhappy with in the context of their relationship, he often told her he couldn't do anything about it until he was in a better position at his job. Morgan believed in the happy-family future picture he had painted for her, and so she overlooked a lot. She rationalized that this was normal— she wanted a successful husband, and they would both have to make sacrifices along the way for them to have the kind of life they were imagining.

    When Morgan came to me, she had found out that her boyfriend's behavior at the infamous house parties was not what she thought it was, and was not what she considered acceptable in their relationship. She was often not invited to saif parties, because her boyfriend assured her it was just the guys. As it turned out, there were girls at the parties in question, just not girlfriends. Not to mention, the sheer amount of alcohol he was consuming at these events had begun to concern her. She wanted me to help her find a way to feel okay about his bad habits now, knowing that they were just related to the stress of his job and would eventually go away when he was promoted and they got engaged, as they had planned and as he often reassured her.

Morgan thought the problem was in her expectations and her inability to be more understanding of the stress he was under. She worked really hard not to overreact and to classify the inconsistencies she was experiencing as harmless, but I could see that Morgan wasn't truly present in her relationship– she was dating the future image he had promised her, not the actual person she was with. My job was just to help Morgan see her current relationship for what it was.

While a relationship with another person is an opportunity to grow together, the core of our connection to our partners isn't found in a future that hasn't happened yet, and furthermore, one that we have no guarantee will ever happen– your relationship is what's happening right now in the present moment. I started by asking Morgan to imagine her ideal relationship— one where she felt supported, loved, seen, fulfilled, and truly, genuinely happy. I encouraged her to be specific by imagining what her life would look like, how she connected with her partner, what values they shared, what their goals were, and how they spent their time. Morgan wrote down the description of her ideal relationship— it was one that involved lots of time outside, weekends together hiking, camping, and traveling, a genuine enjoyment of one another, even in the small moments, a home close enough to the city but not too close, preferably with a dog or two. She wanted a relationship that was encouraging and one where she felt secure. She wanted to have deep conversations and romantic gestures— nothing big, but meaningful.

    I then asked Morgan to consider her current relationship without the promises of a future, just how her experience felt most of the time, right now. She immediately started to explain how her ideal situation just wasn't possible for her current boyfriend yet, but I reassured her this was just an exercise to help her be more conscious of her current reality— she didn't need to defend anyone.

When Morgan described her current experience, to no one's surprise, it was a far cry from what she desired in her ideal relationship. Her current relationship felt stressful, confusing, and she often felt lonely and disconnected, especially on the weekends when he was either unwinding with the boys (read: partying) or recovering from his weekend activities. She loved the idea of the life he was promising her, but it didn't feel like hers. She spent a lot of time wishing that they could build something together rather than feeling like she was waiting around for him to finish what was important to him. And, he often didn't have the time or energy for the deep conversations and camping / hiking trips she really loved.

 I suggested to Morgan that even though she loved her partner, maybe it was possible that she was dating him for everything that he wasn't, instead of everything he was. Of course they had good moments, and of course he had redeeming qualities, but she was staying with him for his redeeming qualities alone. I asked her, "How long are you willing to sacrifice your happiness and fulfillment *now* for something that may or may not happen in the future?"

Morgan paused, tears in her eyes, and responded, "If I leave him now, I'll be alone again. And who knows when I'll find someone else. What's the difference if I'll be miserable either way?"

Gently, I added, "Focusing on his potential is a really good way to ignore bigger issues. People are always showing us who they are and what they value by their behavior, and the longer you stay with a person who does not value you or your relationship, the longer you are keeping yourself from finding someone who does. Right now it's work for a big promotion, but what will it be next year? In five years? There will always be work. There will always be a promotion. There will always be more success to be had... those things won't go away now or ever. So what will be the thing that really brings those future promises into reality? Don't you deserve a partner who can work on his career *and* work on having a good relationship?"

Morgan left our appointment that day with more insight, but not ready to end her relationship. I told her that was not my expectation, at all, rather, I wanted her to commit to staying present in her relationship and prioritizing how she felt in her life right now, rather than using the future as an escape-route from the things that didn't make her feel good. This was Morgan's lesson in conscious relationships.

    She did eventually end her relationship, but it took more time and a little more heartbreak. After breaking it off, she set off on a solo trip across the U.S. to hike some of her favorite places. And guess what? She met someone on a mountain, of all places. It's too early to tell where this connection will end up, but she assures me that she's enjoying herself in the present and working to see him, and herself, for what each of them truly are right now.

    You cannot change the way you date and your love life for the better without deciding to engage in every encounter, every date, and in every relationship with full, present-moment consciousness. Learning to see your interactions with others for what they truly are requires you to see yourself as you truly are– that's what makes it so challenging. Just like Morgan struggled to detach from the future potential she was using to keep her relationship afloat, I couldn't see the dysfunctional situation I was in with Scott with any level of clarity or understanding until I made the effort to see how I had participated in its creation. Conscious dating and conscious relationships aren't only about how you see other people, although that's an important part of it, they're also about your ability to see the role that you play in your interactions with others. This includes all of the deeply held beliefs, fears, and insecurities that dictate how you choose to show up in your relationships– and they all need to be brought into awareness and understood for what they truly are.

  The easiest way to begin to bring consciousness into your dating game is to start with the past. Hindsight, as they say, is always 20/20, and assessing our old dates and relationships can be good practice for becoming more aware in your present and future romances. A good, clear look at what's come before can help you identify some of your own patterns and tendencies. Awareness is key– we cannot shift situations in which we have no awareness. The questions at the end of this chapter will help you get started!

CREATING BETTER LOVE: PRACTICING CONSCIOUSNESS

Consciousness in dating and relationships can be gained by bringing awareness to the parts of ourselves that have the tendency to kick in on autopilot when we're in a relationship. Your goals in bringing consciousness into your relationships are three-fold:

1. We want to assess where we tend to overlook red flags or compromise our standards in the name of lack, an imagined future, or fear.

2. We want to recognize how our own stories, beliefs, fears, and tendencies dictate how we show up in our relationships so we can be aware of them in the future.

3. And finally, we want to gain insight and understanding around how our failed relationships, bad dates, and our romantic past fits into the bigger picture of our growth and expansion.

Get out your journal and make a list of the major romantic relationships in your life. One at a time, ask yourself the following questions about each relationship on your list:

1. In retrospect, what red flags did you ignore about this person or this partnership? What do you wish you had seen at the beginning of the connection instead of later?

2. What things did you hope or believe you could change about the other person? What compromises or sacrifices did you make and how did you rationalize them?

3. In what ways did you talk yourself into a relationship with this person? Did you focus on their potential? Did you ignore glaring differences for the sake of a few things you had in common? Did you focus on one or two important qualities but ignore other unmet needs or requirements? Or something different?

4. What fears or beliefs were triggered with this person that kept you from seeing them or your relationship clearly?

5. What did you learn from this relationship?

6. How could this relationship ultimately lend itself to your growth, evolution, or expansion? How has it prepared you for better, future relationships?

When you've finished this exercise, look back over your answers. What patterns do you notice? What insights did you gain? Use this information to begin to infuse your present and future relationships with consciousness. And the next date you end up on? Be aware of the patterns you noticed and challenge yourself to be honest about the way things truly are, both in yourself and in the other person. Actively pay attention to your intuition– those gut feelings are important input and shouldn't be ignored!

– CHAPTER THREE –
ALWAYS OPT FOR AUTHENTIC

"OMG you're so right. I LOVE libraries too!" I found myself typing.

In my defense, it wasn't a lie, per se, I liked libraries just fine. I love to read, and giant buildings full of books are right up my alley. But the potential beau I was chatting with was *really* into libraries– I mean camping out on sidewalks to protest their closing, regularly donating his money to fund them, and talking about them all the time kinda into them. He was passionate about libraries. Admittedly, I did not love libraries in the same way. But I didn't have any problem alluding to the idea that I might, in fact, have similar feelings so that he would keep talking to me.

It was a pattern I repeated over and over again in my dating life, and so many of us do it without even thinking twice. It may even sound a touch familiar to you. We pick and choose and enhance and diminish parts of our true selves, our personalities, and our interests just like we pick and choose our outfits and shoes for a date. It's like shapewear for our souls, hiding the parts of ourselves we aren't sure are acceptable. We edit ourselves in search of common ground, acceptance, and to make ourselves feel and appear more desirable to another person. Usually, these edits seem like no big deal. They usually don't feel as if they're terribly significant. After all, who was really harmed when I slightly, or even dramatically, exaggerated my love of libraries?

The truth? No one. At least not in the immediate moment. But, what's far more important is what lies behind this seemingly harmless habit of editing ourselves in little ways, and how it affects our love lives in the long term.

First of all, we need to call it what it is—"editing yourself" sounds pretty harmless, but in reality, when we engage in this bad habit we're choosing to be inauthentic. We're choosing not to honor our amazing, unique, divine selves. Far beyond the sheet dishonesty of it all, we are actively saying to ourselves and to everyone else that we aren't good enough as we are. And ultimately, we're setting our potential relationships up for disappointment from the very start.

Library Guy and I only went on two dates. They were good, but not mind-blowing in any way. And in all honesty, how could they have been? We began the interaction based on an edited, inauthentic version of myself that I had presented, but it was the actual-me showing up for our dates. No matter how much I waxed poetic about the merits of public libraries, the energy of inauthenticity permeated every one of our interactions. It may take more than two dates for that energy to affect the quality and viability of your relationship, but it always will in the end. You cannot build a lasting, fulfilling relationship by peddling a not-really-you version of yourself to your potential matches.

The reason the habit of editing ourselves is so easy when it's happening is because it feels like it calms our fear of being rejected by another person. For many of us, the fear of being rejected and not accepted for who we are runs deep and strong. Part of it is biological– we are instinctually wired to want to be accepted and a part of a group. For our ancestors, being a part of the tribe made the difference between life and death. Another part of it is learned– most of us are living our adult lives based on perceptions of ourselves that were formed out of trauma and negative learning experiences from our past. Those past experiences may be obvious to you, and others may not be so apparent, but they're important because they helped shape the way that we think about ourselves and how we relate to the world. One of the first steps to healing the pattern of inauthenticity in your life is to acknowledge and integrate those learning moments from your past and your childhood.

Let me give you an example. When I was deep into healing my bad dating habits, like the pesky tendency I had to edit myself for the sake of acceptance from another person, a big part of my healing process was finding the roots behind the habits. I wanted to know where they came from. I had to ask myself where I learned that I was unacceptable and where I learned that I needed to edit myself in some way in order to find love. I needed to find the places in my past that taught me I was not worthy of love just as I was. And let me tell you, really exploring those questions brought up some deep, deep shit– some of which I never expected.

It was easy to look at my childhood and point to the big, obvious contributors. My parents divorced when I was five, my dad moved out, and I spent much of my childhood yearning for a close relationship with him while he remained largely distant. I knew off the bat that all of the unmet efforts I made as a child to connect with my dad contributed to the deeply held belief that I wasn't enough. But as I continued to sift through the questions I posed to myself, memories came into my awareness that I hadn't expected. Ultimately, I realized that I was holding early memories of shame.

Shame, if you haven't yet been formally introduced to this destructress, is the belief that something is inherently wrong with yourself, as opposed to guilt, in which you believe you've done something wrong. I had picked up shame when I was little– really little. To be clear, some of the memories I needed to address in this process seemed harmless from an adult's perspective. For instance, one of the memories in question revolved around a white, porcelain, cat-shaped night light someone had gifted me when I was four or five. This night light was, to my little self, the most beautiful thing I had ever seen, let alone had the honor of having in my room. I couldn't stop touching it. Late into the night, I would stand up on my bed and touch the cat's delicate little ears– I can still remember how the porcelain felt under my fingers. I was beyond enamored. My parents, understandably frustrated that their toddler would not go to sleep, corrected me each and every time, telling me to lay down and stop touching the night light. Eventually, they took the night-light away, and I was crushed.

    Fast forward to now, as an adult with a toddler, I completely understand wanting my little one to sleep once she's put to bed. I know, as an adult, that a toddler who doesn't sleep is trouble in the making. I know, as an adult, how tired I am at the end of the day after chasing around said toddler and how disheartening and frustrating it is when bedtime doesn't go as planned. As an adult, I can see that my parents were not necessarily being unreasonable. But, as a little girl who only understood that she had, for perhaps the first time ever, something so beautiful and who just wanted to appreciate it, having the nightlight taken away was unfathomable. As I explored that memory and the little girl who experienced it, I realized that as my little-self worked to understand that experience, I had decided on an unconscious level that I must not have deserved that beautiful thing that I loved so much. And suddenly that memory took on meaning that had nothing to do with the nightlight and nothing to do with a toddler who wouldn't go to sleep, but everything to do with a little girl beginning to learn that she didn't deserve good things when she was herself and acted on her authentic feelings.

    That same little girl, just a few months later, would watch her dad pack his bags and leave the house for good. That same little girl, a year later, would go to kindergarten where her teacher would scold her in front of the class for having imaginary friends "at her age". In first grade, she would tell a boy on the playground that she liked him and he would respond by yelling, "Ew!", punching her, and running away. When we follow the pattern and recognize the little moments of learning my younger self experienced, and see how each built upon and re-affirmed the last, you can see how they contributed to my grown-up pattern of editing myself to find acceptance.

    The little four year old girl who had her night light taken away grew into the woman who found herself agreeing to camp out on the sidewalk to protest the closing of a local library, when she knew full well that no part of her was actually interested in sleeping on a sidewalk, library be damned. And, if I'm honest, I already knew in my gut that the relationship was doomed, even though Library Guy was objectively a really great guy.

    These often-difficult memories and the meaning we ultimately apply to them are important for our growth and healing, because they shed light on the purpose of the habit in question. In this case, if making inauthentic adjustments to yourself, your needs, or your preferences is something that sounds even a little bit familiar to you, I want you to understand this: Everything you do, good or bad, you do to solve a problem, serve a purpose, or keep yourself safe. Period, no exceptions. It's how you're wired. I don't want you to think that your habits, self-editing or otherwise, are there by chance, or that they mean you're anything less than an amazing human being. You happen to be an amazing human being doing the best you can at any given moment with the resources you have. And if you have been plagued by the habit of showing up as anything less than your 100% authentic self, know that habit was formed out of helping you meet some need. Somewhere along the way, just like my little inner four year old with her cat night light, you learned that it was safer or better not to be yourself. You learned that your needs for connection, acceptance, belonging, or love were better met when you altered yourself into something you perceived as more acceptable. You learned your needs were better met when you sacrificed your own preferences or feelings for those of another. Everything you've learned to do serves a purpose.

  If we're all honest, we already know that editing ourselves doesn't work in the long run. At some point, the other party will realize that you aren't the person you presented and you will realize that the facade you created doesn't feel good to you anymore– your true self will always prevail, one way or another. It is exhausting and draining to maintain an inauthentic version of ourselves. The tension we create when we craft and try to maintain a secondary version of ourselves is downright difficult because aligned and authentic *always* feels better. It's our fear that convinces us otherwise.

  Sacrificing our authenticity can look like actively trying to be something we aren't, like my own story with Library Guy, but it can also show up in more subtle ways. One of the most difficult lessons in authenticity for myself and my clients to learn has been not betraying ourselves through omission. Not speaking up, not communicating our preferences, not sharing our expectations and boundaries can be equally as damaging as making up things about ourselves that aren't 100% accurate. Years ago, I worked with a client who must hold the record for her streak of remarkably bad first dates. And I mean truly bad– from men meeting her in convenience store parking lots to buy coffee and talk and awkward cafe dates where she struggled to figure out if she should wait in line and order herself or wait for the guy to lead, to plans left too-long unconfirmed and obnoxious driving distances to meet guys who suddenly "didn't feel like eating" and just wanted to hang out at home. She had chalked it up to how bad the dating scene had gotten, how terrible dating apps made everything, and the lack of good single men left in the world.

I, on the other hand, took one look at her and asked, "Why are you agreeing to go on these awful dates in the first place?"

My client didn't really have a good answer. It just never occurred to her that she could set the standard for her dates up front. She so badly wanted something to work out that she was just accepting whatever came her way, in the off-chance there would be fireworks. And she wasn't communicating her needs, preferences, or desires to the men she connected with because part of her just wanted to be accepted. She was taking on the 'cool girl' persona that comes up so often in my work with clients– the erred belief that if we show up to our potential relationships and act like we're good with anything and everything all in the name of not being too much, too demanding, or unlikeable in any way.

When we take on a cool-girl persona as our personal form of inauthenticity, we're letting our fear run the show. Specifically, the fear that we aren't good enough, the fear that we won't be chosen, the fear that our true selves will garner rejection. Even if we aren't actively making up a story about liking something we don't, like in my earlier example, we're leading with behavior that omits who we really are and what we truly desire.

For my client with the record of terrible first dates, I challenged her to lead with her expectations. Instead of waiting for matches and potential dates to set the tone, and then matching it herself, whether it worked for her or not, I wanted her to learn to set the tone. In practice, this triggered big issues of fear for her that we traced back to previous moments of rejection and a childhood filled with moments that she felt criticized for showing her true feelings and voicing her true opinions. She had to learn that she was letting her inner-child run her love life instead of showing up like the powerful, strong, capable, loveable woman that she was. Afterall, even if she were able to pretend her way into a long term relationship, did she really want to spend the rest of her life with a person who only liked a made up version of herself?

Dredging through our fear, shame, and sometimes-painful memories that built the path to creating inauthentic versions of ourselves can be challenging. The fear of not being accepted for who we are, the fear of not being good enough, and the fear of rejection can loom large. I never said it would be an easy habit to break. But in those moments, I encourage you to re-focus on what you truly deserve in love and in life.

You deserve a loving, supportive relationship with a person who accepts you for exactly who you are. You deserve a partner that is truly compatible with you– the real you. You deserve a relationship in which you can be yourself without fear. You deserve a relationship that feels safe, comfortable, and like home because you can be *you*. You deserve to be loved for being who you are.

Making a relationship work by changing yourself, your needs, or your values is like trying on a pair of shoes that don't fit and wearing them anyway, hoping the size of your feet will change the longer you wear them. It doesn't work.

That isn't to say that we don't grow and evolve with our partners, and that isn't to say that when we're in a relationship we don't expand our interests or try new things as we do so. However, the energy behind evolving and growing is light and expansive. That process is born of love, and It feels different than the fear-fueled habit of changing yourself to be accepted or to avoid rejection. Do not fall into the trap of building your love life on a foundation of fear.

When in doubt, opt for authenticity. Understand that doing so is a commitment to practicing something that is unfamiliar to so many of us, and it won't always feel comfortable. But the more you consciously choose it, the more you will realize that anything less feels… awful. You deserve nothing less than to embody your whole, authentic self in every single interaction. And I can assure you, doing so will change the types of people and experiences you bring into your life. Because when we are authentic, and committed to being so, we cannot stay in situations or relationships that are misaligned with who we are.

CREATING BETTER LOVE: SHEDDING LIGHT ON FEAR

If the pattern of editing yourself, even just a little bit, as you engage in relationships and dates is one that you recognize for yourself, I want to invite you to begin to shed light on the root of that pattern. Bringing awareness to the core beliefs and foundational experiences that fuel that tendency is the first step to releasing them and choosing something different. You can start right now.

Our goals in this process are:
1. Discovering the true need behind the pattern. We don't really have a deeply ingrained need to alter ourselves for other people, but that pattern does serve some deeper need. It may be acceptance, love, comfort, or any number of things, but we cannot consciously choose a more aligned way to solve that problem if we don't know what the problem is to begin with.

2. To find the core beliefs and moments of learning from our past. This process allows us to shift our perspective around those old memories that taught us ineffective lessons about the world and ourselves.

3. To look our fears in the face and empower ourselves to learn to consciously choose authenticity because we know that we deserve nothing less.

Get out your journal and explore the following statements. Be honest with yourself and resist the urge to edit or overthink your gut responses. Anything that comes up, even if it seems like a knee-jerk response or doesn't make any sense at first, is valuable information.

1. When is the earliest, very first time you can remember not being yourself, no matter how small or insignificant it may seem? Alternatively, when is the first time you can remember something negative happening because you were yourself (you spoke your

mind, voiced your needs, shared your opinion, did something that felt good for you, asked for what you needed etc.)?

2. Remember that all problems were once solutions. How does the habit of inauthenticity serve you? How does it keep you safe? What needs does it meet? How does it help you ensure you receive what you do want or how does it prevent something you don't want?

3. When is the last time you can remember being totally authentic, without reservation? How did you feel? Looking back, do you hold a positive or negative perception of that time?

– CHAPTER FOUR –
BOUNDARIES, BOUNDARIES, BOUNDARIES

The chef was in the midst of publishing his own cookbook and had an adorable, clean, well-decorated apartment downtown. On our first date, he stopped mid-meal, told me I was beautiful, and still happily obliged when I told him I didn't want to sleep with him on the first date but would be open to cuddling on the couch and watching Netflix. And, miracle of miracles, he respected my decision and didn't even try anything during the movie. I left his apartment with a kiss on the cheek and plans for dinner the following weekend.

He texted regularly, seemed genuinely interested in my life, and was kind and respectful. Sounds like a dream, right?

I know what you're thinking– why is the chapter about boundaries starting off with a story about a guy who seems like he has boundaries in the bag?

I'll tell you why. In fact, it's better we get this gem of a truth out of the way in the beginning, so you can keep it in mind as you read the rest of this chapter: **Boundaries have nothing to do with other people; boundaries have everything to do with *you*.**

It didn't matter that the chef was the perfect gentleman on our first date. It didn't matter that he continued to be nothing short of lovely on our subsequent dates. At that time in my life, I was missing a fundamental understanding of what boundaries were and how they worked. I didn't have good boundaries, and it had less to do with the people I dated, and more to do with the way I navigated my relationships.

When it came to my relationship with the chef, my own lack of clarity around boundaries meant that I was easily swayed by his good manners and the fact that he wasn't trying to get into my pants on the first date. Because I didn't understand what boundaries really were, I confused the basic awareness to open doors and have open conversations about things like splitting or not splitting the check with having healthy boundaries. Dating a man with good manners does not mean you are dating a man with good boundaries. And as for your own boundaries, my friend– they are an inside job.

When your boundaries are MIA, it means you're experiencing every relationship at the mercy of another person's boundaries, whether they're healthy or not. It also opens up the door for unhealthy attachments and a loss of self. Healthy boundaries define your space and make sure that your well-being and best interest are front and center, even in the midst of a relationship. Boundaries are a profound expression of self love– having them in place and knowing exactly what they are is the best way to ensure that the people you're in relationships with aren't disrespecting you, but they also help ensure that you aren't putting yourself into situations where you are disrespecting you.

My own lack of boundaries meant that I fell into the oh-so-common trap of what I like to call headline dating. Headline dating is when we engage in relationship behaviors that sound like the headline of an issue of a trashy magazine— you know the ones: "FIVE WAYS TO MAKE HIM WANT YOU" or "MAKE HIM COMMIT EVEN WHEN HE DOESN'T WANT TO" or "MAKE YOURSELF IRRESISTIBLE AND KEEP HIM FOREVER". Without a strong sense of self and good boundaries, tactics and manipulation can seem like a good way to nail down a relationship. But tactics are a bid for control— we are only driven to use tactics when we seek to control the behavior of other people and the outcomes of relationships we feel unsure in. Boundaries are the tools that empower us to know where we stand in relation to the other people in our lives. When we have good boundaries, we don't need to control others or lose ourselves to ensure we'll receive love.

  The perfectly-mannered chef ended up being quite hung up on his ex-wife of nearly a decade previous, which led to frequent emotional outbursts whenever he was triggered by his past trauma, along with a serious reluctance to commit. His insistence that he "just wasn't ready to settle down" meant that he still wanted to see other people, even after we had been dating regularly for months. His insecurity and trauma driven by his past relationship meant that he also had jealous, passive aggressive outbursts whenever I would talk to or receive attention from anyone that wasn't him. But despite this unhealthy cycle, my own lack of boundaries led to me convincing myself that headline dating was the way to go– from my ungrounded place, I believed that I could influence his behavior, heal his trauma, and make him love me if I were flexible enough, forgiving enough, hot enough, and good enough in every way that he needed me to be.

    This kind of boundary-less dating is based on the belief that assumptions drive expectations for behavior, but we can't assume that if we think, feel, behave, or look a certain way that another person will do what we want or expect. I engaged in this type of behavior for years before the chef actually came along. I compensated for my lack of boundaries and the bad behavior of my partners by convincing myself that if I were more "x" they would inevitably come to their senses and see the error of their ways, ultimately realizing that I was the perfect woman for them. Trying to be the "cool girl" that was refreshing and surprisingly flexible and using manipulative tactics to try and ensure I was liked was actually me living to their boundaries because I lacked my own. My pattern was a direct reflection of my lack of self love and self esteem.

So, in my relationship with the chef, he set the pace and I matched it because I thought that would make me more desirable. When he said he didn't want to commit because he wasn't ready, I said I was totally cool with it. When he didn't want me seeing or talking to other guys, I acted like it was cute when he was protective of me. When he had emotional outbursts about his ex, I comforted him and never pushed him to get help or deal with his issues, or I distracted him with sex. And through all of it, I waved the flag of being the girl who was different from and cooler than all the others. But in reality, I had already lost myself to his boundaries. I wasn't waving my own flag at all, I was just morphing myself into whatever I thought he would like the most.

Then, on a random Wednesday, the chef called me at work. At first, hearing his voice on the other end of the line in the middle of the day was exciting and low-key intimate. I had a passing thought that he was finally coming around to me. Instead, he casually informed me that he had been to the doctor and was diagnosed with chlamydia, and then angrily blamed me for infecting him. I reminded him that I hadn't slept with anyone else since we had met, while he had continued to see other people, but he continued to yell through the phone. He told me he couldn't be with someone who slept around, that I was dirty and a whore, and that he couldn't believe I hurt him like his unfaithful ex-wife had. Emotional and overwhelmed, I stammered that perhaps I had gotten it from a toilet seat (**Pro-tip:** *That's not how it works*). I begged and bargained my way into more time and another conversation– that conversation would drag out for another four weeks. It was four weeks of tension, arguments, antibiotics, and a lot of neglecting my own wants and needs in order to keep a relationship I felt I had invested in.

    A lack of boundaries meant I had let him take over my space. The relationship was built on his boundaries, his wants, his needs, and his values. And all the time I spent molding my expectations and needs to his liking and calling it "being different from the rest" was just a testament to my own lack of self love. I couldn't see my own worth, so I was looking for it in the approval of another person.

You might be thinking that you would never, under any circumstances, put up with what I did when it came to the chef, and you might be right. But sometimes the bargains that we make, the bad behavior that we let slide, and the places that we compromise our boundaries isn't as obvious as it was in this particular relationship. Sometimes it's more subtle or builds over time.

Here are a few questions you can ask yourself to start to explore how you may be in need of boundaries in your love life:

- Do you feel obligated to meet other people's expectations, but then experience feelings of resentment or disappointment when you aren't appreciated enough?
- Do you spend a lot of time or energy imagining or anticipating the other person's thoughts or potential reactions to you or your decisions?
- Are you keeping quiet about things in your relationship that you don't love or make you uncomfortable to avoid

conflict or because you're afraid you'll be rejected if you're honest?
- Do you keep your preferences to yourself, even about small things like how to spend your time together or where to have dinner?
- Do you hesitate to share your true feelings, even when asked, often opting for responses that will keep the peace or you know will make the other person feel better?
- Do you find yourself adopting the other person's interests, hobbies, and social group or abandoning your own?
- Do you find yourself coming up with gestures, plans, or opportunities to make the other person respond in kind to you, especially after time apart or after conflict?
- Do you find yourself facilitating moments in the relationship that you desire, overlooking the fact that the other person isn't showing up or contributing to the same degree you are, while you secretly hope they will?

If you recognize yourself in these questions, or you found yourself saying "yes" to many of them, you may need to re-evaluate the boundaries in your relationships.

In addition to protecting our space from the intrusion of other people, healthy boundaries also help us not inappropriately attach ourselves to other people. Healthy boundaries empower us to take responsibility for our own behavior, actions, and happiness. They keep us from attaching our sense of fulfillment to expectations that we create for another person.

Let me tell you about John. John and I met in middle school. We became friends and he dated my childhood best friend for years. When said best friend moved hundreds of miles away to another state, John and I shared a lot of space in our joint loss, and during our senior year, I realized I had feelings for him— lots of feelings. Since he was still in a long distance relationship with my best friend, he was 100% off the table as far as I was concerned. We graduated high school, parted ways, and I kept my secret.

Fast forward four years and I had graduated from college, survived a pretty tumultuous relationship of my own (more on that later), lost touch with all of my high school friends and connections, and had moved to another state. This particular day, having finally decided to start dating again, I was on my way to a blind date at a restaurant in a town that I had never been to before. Being that this was pre-smartphone and before GPS was an option, I had printed the directions to the restaurant out from mapquest (I'm dating myself, I know), but had gotten lost along the way. I ended up pulling over on the side of the road in the middle of nowhere and calling everyone I knew for directions. When I finally had my bearings and a vague idea where I was headed, I realized that I was going to be woefully late for this date. Not wanting the guy I was meeting to think I stood him up, I scrambled to find the scrap of paper I had written his number on. As I pulled back into traffic, I dialed his number into my cell phone with one hand, keeping the other on the wheel and one eye on the road (Don't text / dial and drive!)

    As I waited for him to answer, I silently reminded myself that his name was Jay and rehearsed what I would say, so as not to sound flustered or awkward.

After a handful of rings, he answered, "Hello? This is John."

I hesitated, glancing down at the paper on the passenger seat again. It was barely legible, but I had definitely written the name "Jay" over the top of the number.

I went with it, thinking I had misheard him. "Hi, is this Jay?"

"No, sorry, this is John. Can I ask who's calling?"

"Oh, yeah, um, this is Kari. I think I have a date with you tonight, but I thought your name was Jay, I must have misheard..."

"Kari?" He cut me off. "Kari from Regional high school? "

"Yes...?" Shit, I thought. I've blown pas awkward when I can't even get his first name right and he somehow knows everything about me.

"KARI, it's John, you know, we went to school together? I don't have a date with you tonight because I'm actually at my own college graduation party, but I'm so glad you called. We should definitely get together."

Yes, you read that right– on my way to a blind date with someone else, I mis-dialed a completely new number and ended up calling the guy I had a major crush on in high school, whose number had not been stored in my phone for years. And, what's more, he wanted to hang out. I didn't know if it was an insane coincidence or a stroke of divine luck.

The blind date I went on that evening is, to this day, one of the worst I have ever been on. After the guy barely spoke and hit on the waitress in front of me, it's only redeeming quality was that John and I did hang out a couple of weeks later. We caught up over nachos and margaritas at a divey bar on the campus of his grad school. I laughed more than I could remember laughing in ages. We sang karaoke and carried each other back to his apartment. Oh, and in case I forgot to mention it– he was single.

From that night on, I spent time with John nearly every week. We went out regularly, we sang way more karaoke than any two people ever should, we talked all the time, we cooked together, watched movies together, went to events together, went grocery shopping together... and yet, we were never actually together. At the time, I was an aspiring artist, and when John moved into a larger apartment, he set up a space for me in his spare bedroom to paint when I was over (which was often). He, entirely of his own volition, went to the art store and bought an easel, canvas, the paints he knew I liked, and a set of brushes and made a space for me to create. Eventually, I found myself in-between apartments after my previously mentioned engagement ended, and I essentially stopped going anywhere else. I never officially moved in, but I was there so much that I may as well have. Nearly every night we would cook dinner, and then I would paint in the spare bedroom while he fell asleep reading on the floor next to me.

    I can sum up my entire interaction with John for you in one evening. After grocery shopping on a Friday night and making Indian food, I found myself, as usual, in the spare bedroom working on a large painting of a person looking out over a snowy cityscape. It also happened to be snowing outside that evening, and halfway through the post-dinner bottle of wine we were sharing, I turned to John, reading on the floor like he always did, and announced, "It's finished."

    John looked at me, and then at the painting. "It isn't finished," he said.

Before I had a second to be defensive or indignant, as I normally would have if some person had told me that my own painting wasn't finished, he jumped up, shoved my coat into my arms, and practically dragged me outside by the hand. We walked to the now snow-covered park across the street. The snow had stopped falling, but the lamp-lined brick pathways that cut through campus glistened with fresh powder. Wrapping his scarf tightly around his neck, John turned to me and said, "Watch."

Using two hands, he picked up a handful of snow and threw it over his head and into the air. Light fluffy chunks of snow broke apart and sparkled as they fell down, landing on his hair, shoulders, and scarf. "The person in your painting, he's outside, in the snow, but there isn't any snow on him. I wanted to show you because I know you like to see imagery before you paint it."

And in that exact, romantic comedy worthy moment, ladies and gentlemen, I fell in love with John from high school.

And who could blame me? The problem was, John from high school wasn't in love with me. But that didn't stop my boundary-less self from attaching a whole slew of expectations, hopes, and dreams to him. I found myself in a place where I put a whole lot of effort, time, and emotions into trying to be the girl that I thought he would want. I kept it up long after I moved out of his apartment and throughout his other relationships and even my own. I kept it up long after I told him I had feelings for him and he very kindly and gently let me know that he didn't share those feelings. Still, his approval of me meant everything. I was *sure* that if I could prove myself good enough, smart enough, and creative enough that he would realize at some point that we were obviously meant to be together.

    The difference between John and the chef is easy to see. There was nothing abusive, angry, or slimy about John. He was nothing short of sweet, supportive, and a really amazing friend, for whom I am deeply grateful to this day. But my lack of boundaries meant that I attached myself to an idea of him and an idea of a relationship that didn't actually exist. I overlooked clear communication that he was not interested in a relationship with me because I was so focused on the potential that I believed was there. John didn't take over my space the way that the chef did, but I tried my best to take over his.

My interaction with the chef is a good example of how I was lacking in external boundaries– I struggled and failed in setting standards and limits for my relationship and what behavior I accepted and didn't accept. I compromised myself while allowing the chef to set the pace for our relationship. I was completely malleable to his whims, mood swings, and desires because I desperately wanted to keep the relationship potential I felt I had invested in. My interaction with John, on the other hand, is a good example of how I was lacking in internal boundaries. I was projecting my own internal fantasy onto another person and unable to practice a healthy level of detachment or self awareness. There was no filter between my behavior and my feelings, no matter what was happening in reality. Both internal and external boundaries are necessary for relational health and for the dating process. Our boundaries are limits on what happens around us and within our relationships, as well as what happens within us and how we respond to it.

It all comes down to this: healthy, clear boundaries are a necessary and profound act of self love. They define your space and let you know where you end and where someone else begins. Good boundaries empower you to be responsible for your own happiness and fulfillment, and to allow other people to be responsible for theirs. Your concept of boundaries is rooted in your own self worth– whatever you allow or don't allow in your relationships ultimately reflects what you believe about yourself and what you believe you deserve.

    Good boundaries – in words and action – are the starting point for you to become a living, breathing incarnation of your true, confident, know-what-you-want self. And moreso, the relationships you'll attract as that version of yourself will far outshine the ones you've experienced based on a place of questionable boundaries. But learning to set boundaries when you don't have a history of healthy boundaries can be a challenge. It took me years to evaluate and really understand boundaries, even after I had realized that mine were severely lacking. Give yourself a lot of grace and understanding on this journey. Know that your boundaries will evolve as you do, and the more you learn about yourself and the kind of relationships you want, the more you will adjust your boundaries accordingly.

Some of us are learning to recognize and set healthy boundaries even though we didn't have a good model for boundaries when we were growing up. That poor model may have come through observing the relational dysfunction of your own parents or caretakers, or from being a part of a family system that did not allow you to learn healthy boundaries by setting and enforcing age-appropriate boundaries for yourself. I often like to ask my clients to consider what kind of boundaries they experienced growing up to get an idea of what foundations they may be working with when it comes to their beliefs about boundaries. You can start exploring your own boundary foundations by asking yourself the following questions:

- Growing up, did you have your own space and were you allowed to have privacy? Was asking for privacy considered disrespectful?

- When you were growing up, what waa the response in your household if you voiced an opinion, need, or feeling that was different from the other members of your household, especially authority figures?

- Did you feel responsible for other people's emotional states, for example, keeping the peace, regularly adjusting your needs or feelings to avoid a particular reaction, etc.

- Did you feel like you had to be or act like something or someone you were not in order to have your emotional needs met? Or, did you have to step into a role that should not have naturally belonged to you in order to have your needs met? (for example, caretaker to a parent or sibling when you were a child yourself)

Exploring questions like these can start to shed light on where your own beliefs and behaviors around boundaries started. For many of us, we learned to abandon ourselves and be boundary-less in exchange for love, acceptance, and approval when we were very young. Then, we transfer those same dynamics to our own adult relationships, often without even realizing it. If you have historically struggled with boundaries, your journey begins here– at the beginning. The places that you learned and observed relationships in real time as you were developmentally learning how to be a human are those setting the stage for your current boundary struggles. By understanding those roots, you can begin to dismantle the lessons you took on as a child and make space for you to learn new patterns. Trust me, this is a process and it takes time and practice, but it is possible.

 As you learn, you'll find it easier and easier to communicate honestly about your feelings and your needs. You'll get more and more familiar with what you actually want, need, and expect from other people in your relationships, romantic and otherwise. You'll learn to keep the promises you make to yourself and keep your projections, triggers, and emotions in check. Your relationships with others and yourself will improve. Boundaries truly are the crux of healthy relationships– if you take one thing from this book to start implementing into your life right away, let it be boundaries.

CREATING BETTER LOVE: SETTING BOUNDARIES

Healthy boundaries are words and actions that empower you to define your space, communicate what is and is not acceptable for you in your relationships, and set a standard for love and respect in both your relationships with others and your relationship with yourself. Think of boundaries like fences, not walls. Fences are really good at defining space and guiding your understanding of where one thing ends and another begins, but fences also have gates. They allow you to choose what you let in and what you do not. Fences also allow for rearranging and adjusting as you continue to grow and evolve.

Our goals in this process are:

1. To reflect on past relationships and where our boundaries were perhaps non-existent or could have used some work.

2. To consider our current and future relationships and areas in which we

could show ourselves more love and more care by strengthening or adjusting our boundaries.

Get out your journal and explore the following questions. Be honest with yourself and strive to see your past and present relationships for what they were and are. Resist the urge to excuse, bargain away, or alter your feelings or the reality of the situation in order to make it look better. In order to set and practice healthy boundaries, you need to be honest with yourself about the relationships that may have been lacking in boundaries.

1. Consider your previous relationships, or even a current relationship, and think of an example of a time that you felt like you were being mistreated. Get specific about who was involved and what exactly the behavior was that made you feel that way.

2. Consider your own expectations. What expectations did you have in this situation or this relationship? What did you think should have happened, or what did you want

to happen and why was it important?

3. How did you communicate your expectations, needs, or desires? (If you did not, this is the place to start! How could you have?)

4. If a boundary were required to help you feel safe, respected, or to prevent this situation or similar situations from occurring again, take this time to write it using "I" language.

"I feel:

_____

_____

when:

_____

_____

because:

_____

_____

What I need is:

_____

_____

_____."

(For example: "*I feel hurt and upset when you don't contact me for days after we've had a date because it makes me feel like I'm not important to you and you don't value our time together. What I need is for you to check in so I know we're both on the same page and comfortable with how things are going.*")

– CHAPTER FIVE –
GET CLEAR ABOUT ALIGNMENT

"Aligned" is one of the spiritual, wellness, lifecoach buzzwords you might feel like you've seen so many times that it's lost its meaning. In reality, and outside of being plastered all over social media, the concept of alignment is deeply important to helping us reach and embrace our potential in love and in life. Part of my hope in this chapter is to reconnect you with the deep, meaningful impact of the concept of alignment. Understanding what is in alignment for you, and what isn't, will ultimately help you develop an internal method of measuring and assessing your experiences, both dates and otherwise, to make decisions with ease.

Everything in your human experience falls into one of two categories- it is either in alignment or in contrast. Both alignment and contrast serve their own unique purposes in our lives, and both are integral to our growth and evolution. Alignment, however, is usually what we want to create more of, and it happens when we are connected to both our deeply held values and an awareness of our greater truth and purpose.

When I tell people the story of AJ, they usually stop me at least twice to ask, again, if this is really a true story. And I assure you, it is. And while AJ was a little misguided (you'll see why in a minute), to his credit, he showed up and gave 110%, and then some. AJ knew what he wanted and he was dating with a goal in mind. There's nothing wrong with that - in fact, I often advocate for dating with a purpose, but the truth is, not everyone will share your purpose. Not everyone will share your idea of the expansive, fulfilling life you're creating. And not every relationship will align with your values. None of those things mean that there's anything wrong with you or what you want, in fact, that's exactly how it's supposed to be. Human beings are wonderfully diverse, unique, and absolutely fascinating– we are not all meant to be or want the same things. The sooner you realize this, the sooner you'll be off and calling in something that *is* aligned for *you*.

    AJ and I were set up on a blind date by a friend of a friend of a friend back in the days of MySpace (You may have heard of it. It was a pretty big deal a long time ago.) We chatted online for a couple of weeks before agreeing to go out, and he picked me up at my house on a warm, Friday evening with flowers in hand and the car door held open. With my flowers, he also gave me a card– as in a classic, Hallmark card complete with an envelope and the little gold sticker on the flap. It said something benign about becoming friends and meeting new people, and I thought it was an odd, but not necessarily terrible gesture. I shrugged it off, politely thanked him, and filed it away as an endearing sign of first-date effort. By all appearances, we were off to a good start.

    I could tell he was nervous. He seemed flustered and a little frantic, and as we pulled out of my driveway, he was quickly telling me that he had planned and completed trial runs on several potential dates. I nearly did a double take. "You did what?" I asked.

"I did test runs on our dates. I wasn't sure which would be the best choice, and I wanted whatever we did to be perfect, so I planned several and tested them out myself."

I was silent– literally stunned. I didn't know whether to be incredibly flattered or slightly concerned.

He continued, "I thought a good idea may be to go to the circus since it's in town. So I went myself last week to see where the best place to park would be, and what time we should get there to get to our seats easily, and what time to leave to beat the traffic out of that part of the city. Do you like the circus?"

By this time, I was already practicing authenticity and honesty in real time, so I slowly shook my head. "I don't, actually. I'm against the animal cruelty and it makes me really uncomfortable." I wasn't sure how he'd react, but it turns out that your date not being on board for plan "A" doesn't matter so much when plans "B", "C", and "D" are already planned and in place.

When he suggested Japanese for dinner and coffee afterwards, I agreed and started to relax. He told me he was going to take me to his favorite place, and as he guided his car out of town and onto the highway, I wondered where we could possibly be going. As we crossed the border into the next state, my anxiety had started to rise. I barely had time to register my feelings of unease, however, because at that moment, he reached across my lap, opened the glove compartment, and...

...pulled out another greeting card.

This was probably the first greeting card that I had ever been handed with which I legitimately did not know what to do. I held it and stared. Could there possibly be a need for two greeting cards on a first date? Had I missed some fancy Cosmo article touting hallmark cards as the next seal-the-deal dating move?

"Open it!" he encouraged me.

I did. It was equally as benign as the first and simply signed, "–AJ".

I placed it with the flowers and the first greeting card in the back seat and briefly wondered what in the name of all things holy I had gotten myself into.

I was relieved, again, when we pulled into the parking lot of an actual restaurant and not a dark back alley where I would have met my untimely death. The restaurant was small and well decorated, but not enough to distract from the third hallmark card that awaited me at our table when we were seated. I hadn't left his side since we had arrived, so I could only assume he dropped it off at the restaurant prior to our actual date. There was nothing in its contents worth describing, and I was again left in a place in which I was not sure whether to be impressed or uncomfortable with the effort he had obviously made.

    Over dinner, AJ enthusiastically described his family, his vision for his life, and goals he had for his future. He told me about his parents and how eager he was to finally bring someone home to meet them. He explained that he already knew he wanted to get married and have children, and the sooner the better. I could tell he was entirely sincere– AJ knew exactly what he wanted. He was dating with much more of a purpose than I had ever realized was possible; in fact, I had never been on a date with someone who was so clearly driven to achieve a singular relational goal as AJ. To some degree, it explained the sheer level of preparation he had put into our date. AJ was looking for the woman he was going to introduce to his parents, and in his mind, if there was any chance I was that woman, he was going to make sure I was thoroughly impressed.

In the middle of my miso soup, I already knew that I was not an aligned match for AJ, nor he for myself. I had not yet learned to date with pure intention and purpose, but even without knowing exactly what I was looking for at the time, I definitely knew I wasn't going to be the keeper of AJ's strong family values nor the bearer of his many, hypothetical children. We did not share a congruent vision for the future— I knew on the first date that we didn't want the same things out of life or love.

There are two key elements of alignment that you need to be aware of in order to create more of it in your love life. The first is this: **alignment begins with you.** You cannot know what is aligned with you and what is not without knowing yourself deeply and intimately. It's through your own self awareness that alignment becomes possible. After all, how can you determine what is aligned for you if you don't know where you stand or where you want to go? That would be like being asked to complete a drawing of a perfect circle without being able to see where the starting point is. Impossible? Technically, no. But probable? Hardly.

From that end, one of the most important elements to consciously dating your way to better love is your own level of self awareness. There is no right or wrong end goal when it comes to relationships. Truly, whatever vision of the ideal relationship you hold for yourself is both correct and possible, all involved are consenting adults. Perhaps you're looking for marriage and a handful of kids. Or, perhaps you're dreaming of someone to compliment your current lifestyle. Maybe you want to live childfree in a great apartment and form a few casual but reliable relationships for fun and companionship. Maybe you really want someone to be a great bonus parent for your children, or someone who is okay with not getting married at all. No matter what you want, whatever it is that you're hoping to call into your experience requires clarity.

There is power in clarity. We tend to have the bad habit of approaching the soul mate search as if it's a formality. So many of us believe that love, marriage, and happily ever after are automatically in the cards for us, if not now, then eventually. Not only does that leave some of us gravely disappointed when it comes to the reality of our love lives, but it also sets us up to accept relationships that haven't even begun to tap into the immense beauty of what we could have if we took a proactive responsibility in creating our romantic realities. Clarity empowers you to see what's aligned with you and your vision and what isn't, without wasting a lot of time. See, it wasn't difficult to know that AJ and I weren't ultimately aligned, and it didn't take the grand total of sixteen hallmark cards he gave me throughout the entire evening, the fact that he yelled at a lane attendant for not being able to accommodate his post-dinner plans of bowling, or that he forced me, against my will, to his empty, furniture-less apartment at the end of the evening for me to figure it out. The date ended with him insisting I sleep over and me calling 9-1-1 when he refused to let me leave. I knew at the very beginning of the date, even without all of the ensuing drama. And, if AJ had listened, he would have known as well, which likely would have prevented his phone call the next day asking me out on a second date (yes, I'm serious).

All issues of questionably mental stability aside, please don't get me wrong– people change and grow, and we all have the capacity to surprise ourselves and to be surprised by others. But that potential doesn't excuse you from doing the work to get clear on who you are and what you're looking for now. From my perspective– the perspective in which it's my literal job to help people like you form lasting, healthy relationships with themselves and others– dating without a clear idea of what you want is reckless and an utter waste of time and energy.

Whenever you find yourself tempted to date aimlessly or making excuses to avoid the work of really knowing yourself, remember the circle analogy. Knowing where you stand and what your objective is doesn't limit the expansiveness or the size or the beauty of the circle you're creating, it just helps you create one that's accurate and looks the way you intended it.

The second bit you have to understand about alignment is that it requires you to participate in an on-going, self-driven process. Finding alignment in your life and your love life isn't a 'one and done' kind of deal. Alignment is a commitment to yourself that invites you to walk down a path of practice– it will require you to develop your skills of recognition as you move through your experiences and begin to take responsibility for what you observe. See, we *love* the idea of alignment, because it sounds magical and serendipitous, but most of us struggle with the practice of alignment because it requires us to be remarkably honest both about ourselves and with others.

You cannot be in the practice of alignment and also accept people, behaviors, habits, or relationships in your life that are misaligned. And once you choose alignment, sweet soul, you will essentially embark on a journey of realization in which God and the Universe will show you the things currently in your life that are out of alignment. In order to continue on the path of alignment, you will be responsible for remedying misalignments as they come into your awareness, and that is where it becomes challenging. The process of alignment will require you to set boundaries, end relationships, evaluate your own beliefs, and set new standards for your own behavior. The process of alignment makes you ultimately responsible for saying 'no' to everything that is not aligned.

There is no alignment without responsibility. One of the reasons that the concept of alignment seems to have lost its meaning across the fairy-dust fueled Instagram profiles of every aspiring coach and guru is because we've collectively fallen into the trap of treating alignment like a big, fat universal magic trick. As if we can think, believe, and meditate ourselves into alignment and skip over the part where we are individually responsible for holding each of our earthly experiences to the standard we're creating.

One of my earliest dating clients came to me in the midst of aimlessly wandering the world of dating apps with nothing to show for it. She was swiping, going on dates, meeting people, and seemingly doing everything "right", but in her words, nothing was sticking. She was smart, funny, kind, and wildly interesting as a person—there was no reason why she shouldn't have been making lasting connections and having quality experiences. As we explored what might be getting in her way, it became really apparent that she was sabotaging her own dating pool.

In addition to connecting with men who represented what she was looking for in an ideal future partner, she was also connecting with men who clearly did not— and not without realizing it. She told me that she knew what she was looking for in a long term partner, but that some of them were so attractive or so interesting to her that even after she realized they weren't a fit or weren't available for a real relationship, she kept seeing them anyway. She claimed it was just for fun or just for a physical connection, but I challenged her on this— rarely do I see women in my practice who are pursuing men "for fun" who aren't also attached, on some level to hoping that those men will change and suddenly want to pursue the long-term relationship those women were originally after. That isn't to say it isn't possible to have a no-strings-attached fwb situation, but if you struggle with attachment wounds or a history of relational issues of any kind, those types of arrangements will likely be toxic for you.

 When we explored my client's attachment to these men she knew were unavailable and not interested in a committed relationship, two themes came up. First, that a part of her was hoping that by being with her they would realize that she was what they wanted and change their minds about committing. Second, another part of her was using the interest, physical attraction, and casual sex as a form of validation. Because she was striking out with the types of men she actually wanted to be in a relationship with, she felt the need to cling to whatever intimacy she felt she could get, regardless of who it came from.

    My goal with that client was to help her see that by dividing her attention and continuing to say 'yes' to connections that weren't aligned with her goals, she was undermining her own success. The longer she spent time, energy, and resources maintaining casual connections with people who didn't want what she wanted and didn't share her vision for the future, the longer she would water down her results. Those casual relationships with no real potential were not in alignment with where she wanted to end up– it's like taking a road trip and getting off at every rest stop along the way just because they exist as an option. Will you eventually get to your destination? Arguably, yes, but it'll take you a lot longer than necessary.

    At the root of her pattern was a long history of worth issues and a deep desire to be accepted. Her need for external validation stemmed from a childhood where she was covertly criticized and undermined by her parents and older siblings. For her, and for many of us, saying 'no' to someone who wants you, even if they don't want you in the capacity you desire, is tremendously difficult. That inner part of us craves validation and acceptance so much that we may put ourselves in situations where we act to our own detriment to get it. We may be afraid that if we walk away from the sliver of intimacy that toxic connection is offering us, there won't be anything else for us. We may be harboring a fear of being alone or a belief that we aren't loveable, which makes any substitute for the real thing seem appealing.

    For my client, it was all of the above. This was a lesson in alignment– we cannot get what we want while simultaneously saying 'yes' to what we don't want. If you're serious about improving your love life, your dating game, or your relationships in general, it is deeply important that you dismantle anything standing in the way of your own alignment. If it brings you closer to what you desire and what you're creating, it's aligned. If it doesn't, it simply is not.

    Alignment in dating requires you to first evaluate yourself, then your experiences and others, and ultimately choose the path that most moves you in the direction of embodying and experiencing more of your values. It requires you to recognize what alignment looks like and feels like for you and then to intentionally create more of that in your life. So, when you find yourself dating the guy you like but aren't thrilled about? Or the guy you could be interested in if he would only change x, y, and z? Or the guy you think you're crazy about but is married and ultimately unavailable? Entertaining those connections only blocks your path to more alignment.

    What *does* seem magical about the process of alignment is the shift that happens after you commit to pursuing what is in line with who you are and what you desire to create. Saying 'no' to the relationships that are misaligned but are also available and comfortable, like with my client, can be much more challenging than we anticipate. It requires us to face our fears about being alone, confront the limiting beliefs and trauma that have kept us in the same relationship cycles over and over again, and ultimately, it requires us to trust that there is more available to us than we ever imagined. That trust requires faith in something we cannot yet see; however, as we commit to the process of alignment, our efforts are always matched. I've seen it happen in my own life and in the lives of hundreds of clients over the years. When we give ourselves permission to drop the fear of being alone and refuse to engage in relationships and connections we know are wrong for us, our faith is met with opportunities and individuals who are more and more in alignment.

Those new opportunities and new individuals won't be brought into your experience without you taking responsibility for choosing to say no to everything – and I mean everything – that isn't in alignment for you. Upholding your end of the bargain in this case creates space for new, better, and more aligned relationships to come into your experience. Dating then becomes a funnel, moving you down a path of relationships and potential partners that are more and more aligned the further you go. There is so much freedom to be found when we can view dating as a function of the process of alignment.

Remember Scott? The fiancé who ended it right before the wedding? The ending of that relationship set me on my own ultimate heart healing journey, and in the two years after he walked out of our home, I dedicated myself to implementing the tools and techniques that I'm teaching you here. In the very beginning of my triumphant return to the dating scene, I ran into Scott at a local bar. After a few drinks, that deep inner part of me that had begged him to stay and was still burned by his insistence that he never loved me was, understandably, triggered. I found myself falling into that old habit of feeling like I needed to earn his approval and love. I wanted him to realize that he had been wrong about me all along. This had been a pattern I repeated throughout my life, but it had never been so blatantly obvious than it was at that moment. I still wanted him to want me, to choose me, and to validate me. Like many of us do, I had inadvertently tied my sense of worth to his approval.

  We finished several drinks over several hours of conversation, and in what was definitely not my proudest moment, I invited him back to my place. That move marked the beginning of a whirlwind five-week romance in which we played house and picked up essentially where we had left off years earlier. And in the span of those weeks, I began to have a deep realization about what exactly I was doing. The truth was, I wasn't interested in recreating the same relationship we once had. I was grateful for all that I had learned, and I knew that relationship was the catalyst for my own journey of healing around love and relationships, but both he and the dynamics of our interaction had not changed. I could see the same old patterns and dysfunction resurfacing. I could feel myself falling back into the same bad habits of overlooking behavior that I wasn't really okay with. I heard myself making excuses for the parts of the relationship that weren't really aligned with what the still-healing version of myself was looking to create. Scott was not an aligned match for me, and on some deep level, I knew it.

But do you know what Scott *was*? He was safe. He was comfortable. I already knew him. I knew I didn't have to worry about whether I was good enough, pretty enough, thin enough, or desirable enough. He was present and available and had proven in just a handful of weeks that his presence could ease the discomfort I had been feeling about being alone. He was showing up and fixing things in my house and doing all the things I wanted a man to do in my life. It was appealing not to have to deal with the stress and anxiety of the unknown that often comes with dating new people and trying to establish new relationships.

As much as I knew the reviving my old relationship with Scott was not what I wanted, there was so much comfort in just settling into familiar patterns.

One night, Scott and I were lying on my couch watching a movie. In the middle of an eye-roll-inducing love scene (you know the ones), he turned to me and said, "I love you. I made a huge mistake before and I shouldn't have left. I regret it every day... can we pretend it never happened and just start our life together over again?"

You know when people are telling stories and they use the phrase, "and time stood still"? I never really understood that sentiment until that exact moment. It really was as if time stood still and the seconds between his confession and my response seemed to stretch on forever. Part of me knew it would be so easy to just say yes and go back to what only a year or so prior I had wanted so badly. The version of me that he left sitting in that house, crying and asking him to reconsider wanted nothing more than for him to choose me again. And another, newer part of me, knew that I could not go back. I wasn't meant to repeat the same cycle over again. If I were truly committed to healing my love life, I needed to make the choice that was most aligned with the future I wanted to create, not the choice that temporarily appeased my emotional wounds.

    As gently as I could, I explained to Scott that I didn't want to start over, and while I cared for him and his well being, I was not in love with him anymore. I apologized to him for anything I may have done to give him the impression that it was a possibility, including inviting him back to my house that night we had reconnected. Scott was visibly hurt, and he left immediately. It was difficult, and I felt awful for having hurt him. But I also felt free and light and clear knowing that I had stood in my truth.

    Looking back, I now know that reconnecting with Scott marked the very beginning of my alignment funnel. It was no coincidence that I was given the opportunity to say 'no' to a relationship that the pre-healing version of me wanted so much. It was no coincidence that I was brought to a major crossroad right at the beginning of what would become my road to finding a soulmate match. I had to say 'no' to Scott to make space for what was coming. And the road to love ultimately brought me into contact with many people I would have to say 'no' to, some directly and some indirectly, as well as people who would say 'no' to me. Making those decisions and having those conversations aren't always easy, and sometimes they are incredibly painful. But when we view them as a part of the process of alignment, understanding that dating is essentially a funnel moving us along a path, it becomes just a little bit easier.

From this perspective, if a relationship doesn't work out, someone rejects you, or you find yourself in the difficult position of having to end it, it has nothing to do with you or your inherent worth or value– it's an opportunity to learn and move further along the funnel to alignment. Your commitment to the alignment of your relationships will be directly reflected in what shows up in your experiences. The more you learn what alignment looks like and feels like for you, the easier it will be to understand whether you're moving forward through the funnel or circling around the same lesson.

Remember, the process of alignment depends on your participation. Start with cultivating a deep understanding of who you are, what you value, and what you desire in your relationships. Then view the process of alignment, learning, and refinement as a beautiful function of the universe– it isn't a magic trick, but it is magical.

CREATING BETTER LOVE: VALUES

Creating alignment in your life and ultimately cultivating relationships that are aligned *for you* is a process that begins with you. It requires you to commit to creating a clear picture of who you are, what is important to you, and what you want to create. After all, you cannot make decisions that move you along the path of alignment if you aren't sure what exactly you're aligning with. For many of the hundreds of clients I've worked with over the years, this begins with values. Your values represent what's important, what matters, and what guidelines you use to evaluate your relationships and experiences. Use the following prompts to help you begin to explore your own values when it comes to relationships.

Our goals in this process are:
1. To begin to explore our thoughts, feelings, and beliefs about what is

most important to us in our lives and our relationships.

2. To create a starting point for our own alignment funnel and to empower ourselves to set basic parameters for our yeses and our no's for the potential relationships that enter our experience from this point forward.

3. To recognize where we may have adopted values that belong to others or have been passed down to us, so that we can begin the process of deciding for ourselves what's important and what might not be.

Get out your journal and explore the following questions. Resist the urge to edit or second guess your answers. You are not tied down to any of your current beliefs or realities, and we are always in the position of accepting the invitation to learn and grow. Knowing where you're starting is, after all, the best place to start.

1. What were your parents' values and beliefs about love and relationships?

How did you know?

2. Which of the above values and beliefs have you adopted? Do they work for you? Do they reflect the ideal relationship you want to create?

3. What elements of a relationship are non-negotiable to you? What would a potential partner absolutely have to know about you, do with you or for you, or value themselves?

4. How or what would you need to feel to know you were in your ideal relationship? How would you recognize it if you were in it?

Use the answers to the above questions to make a list of 20 values you desire to hold for your future relationships– even if they aren't true now or haven't been in the past. Then, narrow that list down to ten. And then five.

Remember that these values can grow and change with you on your journey, but you now have a tool to help you begin to identify what experiences and individuals are aligned with who you are and what you're creating as they come into your life. There is no right or wrong in alignment, only that you are willing to engage in the process fully and authentically.

– CHAPTER SIX –
EXPANSION OR NOTHING

Josh was the first of many drummers I would eventually crush on. I didn't know it at 16, but the relationships of my early twenties would be awash with the drummers and front men of mediocre bar bands. At 16, what I did know was that I was teenage-girl level obsessed with the tattooed, pierced drummer who showed up in, of all places, Sunday morning service at our local church. I sensed that my parents, ever-conservative and leery about would-be suitors, especially those who were both older and with such extensive body modifications, immediately preferred I have nothing to do with him. But the draw was practically irresistible.

If you know anything about 16 year old girls and the swoon-worthy effect of slightly aloof, tattooed musicians, you know that any discouraging boundaries set were essentially pointless. What's worse, Josh and I had near immediate chemistry. We got along, our interaction was easy, and we both loved and played music. To this day, I cannot count the number of people who have told me over the years that they thought we should be together. As fate would have it, however, we spent the better part of many years not at all together. It happened to be that we were never available or single at the same time. He eventually got married, I moved away, and, while certainly not the end of my questionable obsession with boys in bands, that seemed to be the end of my teenage crush.

Years later, after my obsession with questionable musical talent seemed to have died down and I was smack dab in the middle of my own relationship awakening, if you will, I found myself a bridesmaid in my sister's wedding. And who, lo and behold, was also in attendance? You guessed it– Josh. And because I had a not-always-amazing habit of rekindling old connections even when they had no business being rekindled, we spent the entire wedding, reception, and after party reminiscing. He was divorced, and it felt as if no time had passed at all.

The next day, in the middle of particularly boring meetings at work, my phone buzzed. I glanced down, and found myself smiling amidst the drudgery of my office job. Josh, my forbidden teenage crush, was wondering if I wanted to get together and if I happened to be single at the moment. And, for the first time in the near decade since we met, the timing was correct. I was very much single and still very much smitten.

At the time, my immediate reaction was to assume that this was meant to be. What better rom-com worthy love story could I ask for? Surely this was a sign! After years of missed connections, I was about to have a first date that was literally years in the making with a long-time crush. Josh and I joked about how we were "finally doing it" and made dinner plans for the weekend.

"Meant to be" ended up being the shortest relationship of my life. Dinner began as expected–

we picked up exactly where we had left off. Everything we talked about brought us back around to the past. Everything we had in common was what lingered from before. Every commonality had expired years ago. While the reminiscing had gotten us to exchange a few candid text messages and actually embark on a proper date, it wasn't enough to sustain an ongoing interaction. By the time there were only a couple of wine glasses left on the table, Josh was putting an end to any future explorations of a relationship.

    Admittedly, I was hurt. It felt as if the same insecurities that had plagued me as a teenager had resurfaced. I had a crush on someone cooler than me, and he was rejecting me. Old wounds about not being chosen and not being good enough (and cool enough, and liked enough, and pretty enough) flared up, and I struggled not to cry in the middle of a very nice restaurant. He shared with me in the next moments that he was also experiencing old feelings of inadequacy– he didn't feel as if he was in a place in his life to do the idea of being with me justice. He had spent so many years putting a potential relationship between the two of us on a pedestal that it now seemed unattainable and impossible from his current position.

The truth was, our current interaction, short lived as it was, only worked with the versions of us from many years ago. Everything that we talked about, laughed about, and did together was rooted firmly in the past, and neither Josh nor I were the same people we were back then. At that moment, we were both presented with the choice of repeating the past and trying to build a future from it, or to commit to our own forward momentum. It was so easy to romanticize a relationship with Josh based on our past and based on a version of myself that no longer existed, but even then, I knew on a deep level that I was looking for nothing less than expansion.

Chances are, you've probably had one (or several) experiences of romantic interests from your past resurfacing at one time or another. It isn't uncommon, and I cannot make a sweeping generalization that rekindling connections will always lead to a failed relationship– in fact, I'm sure that isn't always true. But the importance of this story doesn't lie in the detail about a person from the past popping up at a seemingly opportune time, it lies in the idea of expansion.

One of the hallmarks of better love is its uncanny ability to be expansive, and I encourage you to settle for nothing less.

Let me explain– Your relationships, at least the ones in which you choose to invest time, energy, and resources, should encourage your growth and evolution. Your relationships should add to your experience, not take away from it. And the relationships you choose to keep should never limit you to a version of yourself that you have outgrown. Your life should feel richer, more abundant, and more magnificent as a result of the relationships you choose to allow into your experience. Genuinely good and healthy relationships will both add to what you've created and support your continued expansion.

For me, the concept of expansive relationships proved to be a difficult one to integrate into my dating life. See, holding our relationships to the standard of "nothing less than expansive" challenges our deepest beliefs around worth and value and calls us to be selective in whom we allow ourselves to invest time and energy. It forces us to prioritize ourselves in each of our relationships and holds us accountable for not only the standard of our interactions, but also the standard of our own behavior. We cannot expect other people to show up as expansive forces in our lives if we are not willing to expand.

If you struggle with codependent tendencies— aka an "I'm only okay if you're okay" mindset— often marked by approval seeking, a low concept of self worth, fear of abandonment, or a fear of being alone— choosing a standard as high as expansion in your relationships might feel really difficult for you too. In my earliest relationships, I had stepped onto the dating scene as a teenager who had seemingly all of these codependent issues, and I brought them into each of my connections thereafter. It was increasingly challenging to focus on the idea of expansion, for myself or for my relationships, when I lived in a place of constant fear that I would be abandoned, rejected, or not chosen by my potential partners. Because I had not yet learned to believe in my own inherent worth and value, almost any positive attention felt intensely gratifying. This was because any positive attention I received was meeting a need in myself that had nothing to do with my adult-self in search of love and everything to do with my wounded inner child.

As a child, I struggled with trauma around the sense of being abandoned, as well as beliefs that I had to prove I was good enough to deserve love. I did not grow up with a healthy concept of worth and value. I often felt alone, overlooked, and unimportant to the people I cared about the most as a child, and I became hypersensitive to those feelings in my adult relationships. That cycle of low self worth, earning love, and fear of being abandoned translated into a love life in which I was constantly seeking approval that I wasn't sure I actually deserved. It is intensely difficult to hold high standards for our relationships when part of us isn't sure we even deserve to be loved in the first place. Ultimately, I accepted behavior that was far less than what I should have entertained, because on some level, everything felt like it might be more than I actually deserved.

Sometimes, relationships that aren't on the expansion track are easy to spot, like my short-lived relationship with Josh. That singular date was more about closing a circle on my past than supporting any version of my future. Add to that list the boyfriend who was angry that I applied to grad school because it would take up too much time; the relationship in which my beau threw a television across the apartment because that particular night, I wanted to go out with my friends instead of him; the two married men who weren't, and never would be, available; and the minister I dated only because I thought my parents would approve. Anytime we are compelled to start, stay in, or entertain a relationship out of fear or the expectations of others, we are settling for less than expansion and less than what we deserve.

Other relationships may not feel expansive for more subtle reasons because the triggers may be rooted in childhood beliefs, behavior that part of you has come to accept as normal, or simply because it doesn't seem 'bad' enough. Perhaps you've learned to interpret possessiveness as a form of love, rather than an attribute based on fear, expectation, and dependency. Maybe you've become so accustomed to not feeling like a priority to your dates and romantic connections that you permit behavior from others that you should not. Or, maybe like me, you've become so caught up in the process of seeking approval from your potential matches that you fall into the trap of losing yourself every time you make a connection that seems to fill that need. These types of indicators on the expansive-scale can be more difficult to see because they're often part of long-repeated patterns that require deep introspection and healing to sort out.

As you move into a space of accepting nothing less than expansion in your relationships and you hold the expectation that your interactions will add to your experience in some way, you'll get a lot better at recognizing the signs when a particular relationship just isn't it. As you get clear on what expansive means to you and feels like to you at any given moment, you'll be better equipped to recognize everything that does not feel that way. It will become nearly second nature, and you'll recognize limiting, constricting vibes like a bad smell in the fridge. And the more you practice holding this standard in your relationships, the less patience you'll have for anything less than that.

I recently worked with a client, Lynn, who had originally booked a session with me because she wanted help navigating the anxiety she was feeling in her relationship. She assured me over and over again how wonderful her partner was, but he was very busy with work and sometimes wasn't as available as she would like him to ideally be. She recognized that her anxiety about his availability or responsiveness was her own, and wanted to work on managing it. We dove right in, with the benefit of being able to explore her relationship dynamics and her responses to them in real time.

The more we explored, however, the more it became apparent that Lynn believed the responsibility for responding, changing, and adjusting in her relationship was hers alone. Not only did she spend a lot of time and energy justifying the decisions and behaviors of her partner, she continued to find fault in herself for needing and wanting anything more or different. While I thought there was value in Lynn learning to self soothe and manage some of her anxious responses, I also focused on helping her realize that her desire for connection, courtesy, and more time and attention from her partner weren't wrong. And, in the instances where he wasn't available or responsive for long periods of time, feeling confusion, hurt, and even anxiety wasn't wrong or even misplaced.

As I continued to encourage and support Lynn in building resiliency, I also encouraged her to begin communicating with radical honesty what she was feeling and needing in her relationship in real time. I explained that her partner's response to active communication would be information in itself, and she deserved a relationship where she could experience growing intimacy, understanding, and security as her partner understood her needs and triggers. While he wasn't responsible for her feelings, he should be responsible for his behavior and not want to cause her to feel badly if it was in his control not to. To her testament, Lynn was so brave as she practiced new skills and remained open to the feelings that came up in the process. With the right support and tools, she was able to show up in her relationship more authentically and ask for what she needed. Her partner, on the other hand, was not appreciative of Lynn's new skills. He responded by pulling back, criticizing her emotionality, and even gaslighting her into believing that her unmet emotional needs were actually her own fault, not his responsibility. He had no interest in adjusting their dynamic, and even though he didn't say that, even Lynn could see that he was showing that through his behavior and actions.

I asked Lynn if she thought she could be happy and fulfilled in this relationship dynamic— the ultimate choice as to whether this relationship remained a viable possibility for her was hers alone to make. She hesitated, and I asked her to just think about it between sessions. There was no rush to make a decision immediately, but I also challenged her to make her decisions based on the reality she was experiencing now, and leave any promises, potential, or futures where she could imagine things being different out of it. Staying in a relationship for everything it wasn't but could be was not healthy and wouldn't serve her in her present situation.

When Lynn came back to her next session, she shared with me that she and her partner had decided to take a break. She didn't feel ready to end it entirely, but she wanted to take some time to reevaluate, reconnect with her friends, and focus on herself. As it turned out, during her break Lynn reconnected with an old friend who was also single. He was the embodiment of secure attachment, and over the handful of plutonic dinners they had, Lynn experienced something she had started to think wasn't possible— she wasn't anxious, even though she was attracted to him. He was kind, attentive, and responsive, even though they were only friends. They had great conversations, great natural chemistry, and his presence and ability to hold space helped her also feel more comfortable being genuinely present in the moment. In her own words, when she was with him she felt like more of herself, but better. As she described her time with her friend to me in our subsequent sessions, I challenged her with this: "If someone who is just a friend can be this considerate and attentive, this mindful of your feelings and needs, and create spaces where you feel calm and entirely yourself, what makes you believe that you shouldn't be able to expect the same from your partner?" Lynn didn't need to leave her partner and start a relationship with her friend, but she could use their interaction as a model for what was possible. I asked Lynn what her life and relationships would be like if she committed to using the quality of her feelings as the standard in her life. She didn't know, but she was starting to see that maybe her needs mattered, and maybe she had been clinging to a relationship with a person who was either unable to or uninterested in meeting them. And maybe she deserved better.

Lynn began practicing prioritizing her own needs and feelings, using how good and secure she could feel as the measuring stick for the people and experiences she allowed into her life. And after some time, she recognized that her relationship with her current partner didn't meet that standard. She ended the relationship, and as I supported her through the breakup, Lynn realized that she had made every effort to make that relationship work. She knew she was growing and evolving and that her connections needed to be able to support that, and moreso, encourage it! After an appropriate amount of time, Lynn did end up connecting with her securely-attached friend romantically, and while no relationship is ever perfect or free of triggers and conflict, their relationship has become a beautiful container where both of them feel supported and safe enough to expand and grow through any differences or difficulties.

As I started to heal my own childhood wounds and triggers, I stopped showing up on dates and in my relationships from a place of fear, hope, and expectation. I learned to hold my potential partners to higher standards of behavior, rather than wondering if I was meeting theirs. I tolerated less, and the caliber and quality of my relationships shifted upward. The qualities and values I looked for in potential partners became more and more specific. Enter Steve, a handsome, successful and attentive executive I met online, who I found myself very much interested in.

On paper, Steve seemed like a dream. He had his shit together, for lack of a better term, he was very masculine in a way that made me have all the feelings, and he was very, very attractive. Steve was also very attentive, which spoke volumes to my inner child who was used to feeling ignored and neglected, and on the surface seemed really sweet. We dated over the span of several weeks, but the longer we spent time together, the more intrusive Steve became. His text messaging became more and more frequent, the questions he asked became more and more overbearing, and he started taking on the responsibility of making all of our plans. Chivalrous? At first, perhaps, but it quickly became apparent that Steve had a bit of a possessive, controlling side. He wanted to be able to make plans for us without asking, he expected to know where I was and who I was with all of the time, and he absolutely would not tolerate me dating or talking to any other men, even at the very beginning of our interaction. He also had a very annoying tendency of speaking over me and ignoring my opinions and input unless they aligned with his own, and then feigning ignorance whenever I confronted him.

Still, I continued to date Steve. He was a dream on paper, remember? He was future oriented, successful, and handsome. It was not difficult to imagine him taking me off the dating market permanently, and likely with a big, fat diamond ring. And then, because the universe sometimes likes to choose the most random moments for our biggest realizations, I had an epiphany. Specifically, I had an earth-shattering epiphany over sushi in a very upscale restaurant about what I was allowing in my relationship and how it actually made me feel.

While perusing the menu, I mentioned to Steve that all of the rolls on the menu sounded great (they did), but that I didn't like eel.

Steve looked up from his menu, and with a touch of incredulousness, replied, "You don't like eel? Eel is great."

I shrugged in response. "I don't like it. I never really have. But if you want it, we can order separately."

"You probably just haven't had good eel. I'm sure you'll like it if we get it."

"Oh, it's okay, I just don't want eel. I'll just order rolls without it if you want to have it. It's not a big deal." I had decided to stick to my guns over the eel issue. I genuinely didn't want to eat it, and I could not understand why he was making such an issue over it.

Steve peered at me over his menu, assured me that it was totally fine, and told me he was fine ordering the rolls that didn't have eel so we could order together. "This restaurant is amazing," he assured me. "Whatever we order will be delicious. And besides, I'm here with you, which is what I really want anyway."

I smiled and settled back into my seat while he ordered. I loved that he always ordered for us. It seemed so intimate and decisive, and Steve was spectacular at making me feel cared for.

When our food came, we busied ourselves with soy sauce, ginger, and conversations about work and the weekend ahead. He had made plans for us to have brunch on Saturday and see a show later that weekend. For a moment, I caught myself thinking that this must be what a real relationship is like. We had just started on our sushi, which was as delicious as he had promised, when Steve looked up from his plate and asked how I was enjoying dinner.

I smiled at him. "It's amazing, and this really is a great restaurant. Thank you so much for introducing me to it."

Steve paused, and asked again, "So, you like the sushi?"

I chuckled, "Yeah, it's really great."

Nonchalantly, he gestured at two of the rolls with his chopsticks. "These two rolls have eel in them. I told you you'd like it. I'm glad to see I was right."

And in that moment, the universe walloped me with that epiphany I mentioned earlier— Steve was actually an ass.

Sure, he had it together, but he was only supportive to the degree that it allowed him to be controlling. I felt seen with him because he happened to be attentive in his methods of control, not because he truly saw me, valued me, or heard me. And, ultimately, I realized that I didn't feel expansive with Steve. I felt like a child. I felt small, disregarded, and like an accessory to the life he was creating. It struck me that I would never be a partner to Steve, whether he was manipulating me by ordering food I had communicated I did not want to eat or making plans with the expectation that I would be there simply because he wanted me to.

Then, dear reader, with quickly rising shock and anger, I made the most dramatic relationship exit you could possibly imagine. To this day, I have never topped this level of drama.

Knowing it was over, I looked down at my plate, placed a hand at my collarbone, and looked up at Steve with wide, tear-rimmed eyes. (I had mastered dredging up tears on demand as a teenager with undiagnosed ADHD and a penchant for turning in assignments late, combined with a strong fear that my parents would find out) He looked at me expectantly, and all but shaking with anger, I took a quick, shallow breath and said, "Steve..."

Perhaps feeling the weight of what was coming, Steve put his chopsticks down and sat back in his chair. "Kari, what's wrong? Are you really mad about the eel thing?"

"[Insert dramatic pause]... I'm allergic."

The rest of our time at the restaurant can only be described as the most Oscar-worthy performance of my life. Had you been there, you wouldn't have questioned my imaginary moderate, but potentially life threatening eel allergy for even a second. And Steve certainly did not. He panicked when I claimed difficulty breathing and tightness in my throat, apologized every time I coughed or wheezed, and was absolutely torn up by my tears. He tried several times to get me to lay down on the floor or call an ambulance, but instead I insisted he take me home immediately.

    I laid in the backseat of the car and let him drive me home amidst a chorus of apologies. When we pulled into my driveway, still teary-eyed, I lectured him on the importance of really listening to other people and respecting their wishes, especially when you hadn't been dating them long enough to actually know everything about them. I told him how hurt I was that he put his need to be right over my physical safety, even if it wasn't completely intentional. And I explained that I didn't want to continue dating, even though I was sure he'd no doubt make some other girl very happy. Steve apologized a seven-hundredth time and drove away, hopefully having learned a hard lesson about listening to the people he wanted to keep in his life.

In retrospect, my performance wasn't entirely necessary, but it was very satisfying in the moment. What I want you to take away from this chapter is not how to terrify a questionable date within an inch of his life, but that you have permission to raise your standards. No matter how good a relationship may look on paper, no matter how much you may think you "should" settle, or how much your girlfriends may tell you you're being too picky, it is your inherent right to expect nothing less than expansion from your relationships. That isn't to say everything will be conflict and difficulty free, but there is a distinct difference in facing difficulty with someone who is supporting, loving, and a catalyst to your growth and evolution than with someone who is not.

Chances are, you're probably able to look back at your relationship history and name at least a few connections that didn't feel expansive to you for one reason or another. And, chances are, you're probably wondering how you're supposed to know if a relationship actually is expansive or not– at the end of the day, what 'expansive' looks and feels like is up to you. Only you can identify what you need to feel like a relationship is supporting and expanding your experience, but it does involve the joy and beauty of being in a relationship in which both you and your partner encourage each other to grow, evolve, and become the best versions of yourselves. When you are able to show up in your relationships as your full, whole, healing self, and give your partner permission to do the same, your love can be the catalyst to an experience that opens you up to all life has to offer with excitement and passion.

If you find yourself struggling to define what is expansive in your life and what is not, let me offer a few guidelines when it comes to love. As you read through them, notice which statements resonate with you, notice which statements remind you of past relationships or patterns you may be carrying in your love life, and notice which statements trigger specific thoughts, emotions, or memories.

1. Expansive love is not based in fear
2. Expansive love is not possessive and does not rely on control
3. Expansive love is not restricting or suffocating

4. Expansive love does not limit you to a past version of yourself that you have outgrown
5. Expansive love does not leave you feeling anxious, unsure, or confused
6. Expansive love has your best and highest interest in mind
7. Expansive love honors your needs
8. Expansive love makes space for you to be yourself, while rooting for your full potential
9. Expansive love is encouraging and supportive
10. Expansive love encourages you toward growth
11. Expansive love awakens us to our most authentic selves
12. Expansive love is free of demands and expectations
13. Expansive love is grounded in the notion of your inherent worth and value

CREATING BETTER LOVE: EXPANSION

Only you can determine what aspects and elements of a relationship would feel expansive to you. Instead of viewing this as pressure or another thing you have to figure out, think of the process of identifying what is expansive as an opportunity to dream. Get excited about the potential you can create in your future relationships! You deserve nothing less than a connection that adds to your experience and helps you embody the best version of yourself at every turn– and you get to use this time to imagine and manifest exactly what that might look like.

Our goals in this process are:

1. To get in touch with the essence of expansiveness and create our own personal definitions of expansion.

2. To create a vision of expansiveness to help us tune into the feeling that our future, ideal relationships can hold for us.

3. To identify ways that we can bring the energy of expansiveness into our own lives as we make space for relationships to do the same.

Get out your journal and explore the following questions. Resist the urge to edit or second-guess your answers. Remember, your definition of expansiveness is yours alone. You have permission to dream and imagine in big ways, there are no limits to what you can call into your experience.

1. Think about the word expansion. Some synonyms include: growth, evolution, amplification, embellishment, enhancement, gain, boost, and bonus. Have you ever felt expansive in your life before, even if it was short-lived or a little bit? What made those moments feel expansive to you? What made them stand out from the rest of your experiences?

2. Imagine you are experiencing your ideal, forever relationship, without limits or reservation. Imagine the details of your life and how it feels to be in this future relationship. How would your ideal relationship bring expansion into your experience? How would your ideal partner support your growth? How would your

interaction add to your life?

3. Look over your answers for the first two questions of this section. How can you bring feelings of expansiveness into your own experience as you make space for your ideal relationship? List specific, tangible ways that you can make your own life feel more expansive.

– CHAPTER SEVEN –
IT'S ALL ICING ON THE CAKE, BABY

When I set out to write this book, I had no intention of including my relationship with Tom. In part because it could probably make up an entire book by itself, and in part because it is difficult to write about. Much of my personal journey in healing my relationship patterns and love-life issues centered on healing the trauma from this relationship, and it seemed much more comfortable to keep it private. But, as I outlined this particular chapter, I kept coming back around to this story. No matter how many other examples or stories I tried to put in this chapter, nothing seemed to fit. As I write this, I am choosing to remain faithful to what I believe I've been called to share, no matter how difficult it may be. Somewhere out there, someone may read this book– perhaps it's you– that is looking for freedom from a damaging, all-consuming relationship. And this chapter just might help a little bit.

In this case, I'll start with the end.

I had been with Tom for just over a year. We lived together, ate together, went everywhere together, and did everything together. From nearly the moment we met, our connection could be described as nothing less than consuming. A year into our relationship, I was asleep in the bed that we shared when Tom violently shook me awake. He was sitting on the edge of the bed, calling my name, hands on both of my shoulders. As I came out of my sleep, I immediately thought something was wrong– as in, the house was on fire or there had been a medical emergency or a break in. What I wasn't expecting was for something to be very wrong in my relationship.

Tom told me that we needed to talk. I glanced at the clock– 3:37am. I was confused and exhausted, but agreed, assuming that the conversation must be incredibly important for him to wake me up at such an hour. At my slow nod, Tom launched into the expected platitudes. He loved me; I was beautiful and amazing; it wasn't me, it was him, and so on. It took me several minutes to understand that he was breaking up with me. At nearly 4 in the morning. On a Monday.

In short, he had been up all night thinking about it and had decided that our relationship was no longer the thing that did it for him. He claimed he no longer felt that same level of deep connection he had felt in the beginning. He explained to me that God had told him it was time to move on. He explained that he needed to find the right person for him, the one God intended for him to be with, and I needed to do the same.

And, he wanted me to leave at that exact moment– at nearly 4 in the morning on a random, rainy Monday.

I don't remember feeling anything but shock. I was in so much shock that I didn't even question him when he told me to get up and get dressed. I didn't push back when he handed me two black trash bags and told me to collect my things. He sat back on the bed and watched as I put clothes, shoes, jewelry, and a year's worth of a life into two bags. When I asked him where I was supposed to go, he shrugged. When I asked him why he was doing this, he told me it was because he loved me and wanted what was best for both of us. When I asked him if we would still be friends, he said, "Of course."

It was now 4:30 in the morning. Tom walked me to the front door of the house we had shared for the past year. He didn't offer to carry my bags and he made no gesture of affection as I walked out. In fact, as I stepped out onto the step into warm, damp air, Tom closed the door behind me without a moment of hesitation. I heard the dead bolt slide into place before I had left the landing.

To this day, there have been few moments in my life that compare to that moment. I found myself standing alone and locked out of the place I thought of as my home, while the person I believed loved me more than anything was the one who had locked the door. I genuinely had never seen this coming. In fact, at any time previous to that early Monday morning, I would have sworn that Tom would be with me forever, without question— we had settled into that inseparable, can't-do-without connectedness. It seemed like everything I wanted and needed in a relationship, which now I know was just to be completely wanted and needed in my relationship.

    When we met, I was immediately enthralled by the level of attention and need he seemed to have for me. Tom wanted to be with me all the time. He wanted me to do everything with him and never wanted to be apart. He wanted to know where I was and who I was with, at all times. He waxed poetic over our deep, immediate connection and claimed that the reason he got upset when I did things that didn't involve him was because he loved me so much and couldn't bear to be apart from me for very long. I could feel his anger simmer whenever another guy paid attention to me, and I told myself that it only demonstrated how much he wanted me. Every time Tom told me he needed me, it was as if my purpose in life had been renewed. I was important. My inner child seemed to be in all her insecure glory— I had spent my entire childhood and adolescence feeling ignored, unseen, and not good enough. So, it was no surprise that in the beginning, this relationship felt like everything I had ever needed.

    Like many relationships before, and sadly many after, I let this sense of connection and chemistry overtake my entire life. It wasn't necessarily dramatic, it wasn't all at once, and it certainly wasn't what I consciously realized I was doing at the time, but I slowly allowed less and less time, energy, and resources to be devoted to the things that I loved. The things in life I was passionate about fell to the wayside. The relationships I had with my friends and family, my professional pursuits, school, and anything that wasn't my relationship paled in comparison to how Tom made me feel. So great was my internal need for external validation that I practically gave up everything at the first sign that need might be met.

    That Monday morning landed me smack dab in the middle of an immediate and deeply difficult realization— I had given up so much of my own life and autonomy that I didn't even know where to go. My relationships outside of my romantic relationship with Tom had deteriorated to the point that I didn't feel I had any other connections to fall back on. And while sleeping in my car the rest of that night and the next was difficult and deeply humbling, the bigger, more difficult realization would take a little longer to land– It wasn't just that I didn't know where to go that night, I didn't know who I was anymore. I had enmeshed and ultimately lost my identity in my relationship with Tom, to the point that once it was removed I was left with no internal sense of self, no inner balance or direction, and no idea how to recover.

 My post-Tom self wasn't much more than a shell of a being. After sleeping in my car for two nights, the black trash bags that contained all of my things taking up the entire back seat of my tiny hatchback, I went back to my parent's house. Over the next year and a half, I struggled with the consequences of my all-consuming relationship with Tom. My grades had dropped and I found myself on probation at school. The relationships with my friends and family were in deep need of repair– repair that would take years to complete. I was depressed, anxious, and pursuing very regular therapy and the necessary medication in order to function. I lost my job and my 20-year-old self spent a lot of time holed up in my parent's basement painting and journaling like an angsty teenager. Throughout that time, I also endured angry phone calls, sporadic text messages, and strangely misplaced love letters in the form of emails from Tom.

After a full two years had passed, I finally felt okay enough to go on a date. Through my parents, I had met a kind, quiet man who also happened to be a professional balloon artist (yes, I'm serious. That is a real thing, apparently). Though I'm sure my parents hadn't considered that we might date, he was creative and interested, as well as gentle and unassuming in a way that my soul probably needed in order to be able to wade back into the dating pool. On our first date, Balloon-guy and I had dinner and spontaneously drove to the beach. We walked along the shore and I spilled my guts about Tom and how long it had taken me to even begin to recover from that relationship. (PS- I do not recommend lamenting about your exes on a first date- or second date for that matter. I didn't know better yet!)

I stood at the edge of the water, waves lapping my feet and fighting back tears, when this sweet man put his hand on my shoulder and gently suggested that Tom was, in fact, abusive, and I was, in fact, a victim of his abuse.

In hindsight, he was right. Years of healing, personal development, professional training, and getting crystal clear on what is appropriate in relationships and what is not have enabled me to look back at my relationship with Tom and see that he was, without question, abusive. I could have left it at that. But here's the thing– if you really want to heal your heart, get free and clear of your relationship past, and consciously create better love in your life, you must take responsibility for any part of your relationships that is yours to take. There is no excusing abuse, ever. However, that doesn't mean that I didn't play a role in my relationship with Tom, and it doesn't mean there were no lessons for me to learn from that interaction.

Abuse aside, my relationship with Tom revealed a big, problematic pattern I had in all of my relationships up until that point. My insecurity, childhood trauma, and beliefs about love meant that I had been using my relationships as the ultimate form of external validation. I hadn't run screaming from Tom's massive red flags because his possessiveness and control looked like love. Tom made me feel needed, wanted, and important from the broken perspective of my inner child. I had learned to approach my relationships as if each one held the answer– the answer to my lack of self worth, the answer to my purpose in life, the answer to making me feel secure, safe, loved, and worthwhile. I had a deep belief that finding the right relationship would be the ultimate sign that I was okay, that I wasn't broken or less than, and that I deserved to be loved.

  But I had it all backwards. Our relationships were never meant to withstand the pressure of the expectation of total fulfillment. The more stable our inner sense of self truly is, the less likely we are to lose ourselves in situations like I did in my relationship with Tom. That isn't to say that we don't need relationships with others, or that we are ever intended to be isolated in any way. It is only to say that the more we learn to find our validation, sense of worth, sense of value, and sense of love from within, the more our relationships can rise above our basic needs of self-fulfillment and add to our experiences in really gorgeous, meaningful ways.

Your relationships are meant to be the icing on your really worthy, beautiful, unquestionably valuable, absolutely divine cake. Your relationships are meant to add to what you've already built and are building. Your relationships are meant to beautify and ornament the foundation that you have already invested in. And the stronger your foundation, the more beautiful the icing that you invite into your experience can be.

Once upon a time, long before I was blessed with the amazing job of being a relationship and dating coach, I tried my hand at professional baking. My roommate at the time, who is now a very accomplished and widely recognized professional pastry chef, and I were binge watching one of those custom cake shows that were wildly popular at the time. Part way through several bottles of wine, we looked at each other and said, "We can do that." The very next night, we ran to the grocery store, bought a bunch of supplies, and made our first carved, custom cake. It was beautiful, honestly, but we had a lot to learn about cake creation– including the fact that the icing on your cake, whether traditional buttercream or complex fondant, is only as good as the cake it adorns. In order to support the complex, beautiful edible art we were creating, the cake itself had to be a certain density, temperature, and texture. And it needed to taste as good as it looked!

Your relationships are like this— in order to support the gorgeous, better love relationship you desire, your cake needs to be on point. (*Psst— the cake is you!*) You need to invest as much, if not more, time, energy, and resources into your own wellbeing and healing as you do into securing your forever relationship. Because no matter how beautiful that perfect match person may be, if your internal foundation isn't there, if you haven't paid attention to your internal state and taken great pride and pleasure in creating a life for yourself, the connection will not be sustainable.

The pattern of using relationships as a source of validation and a total foundation manifests in three ways that I often see in my practice:

1. **Loss of Self:** The first is the tendency to lose one's sense of self once in a relationship. These relationships, even if they aren't abusive like the example

I used, tend to move very quickly and feel all consuming. They cause us to lose sight of the other things in our lives and usually burn hot and fast.

2. **Expectation of Fulfillment:** The second shows up as the belief that the right relationship has the ability to bring fulfillment, happiness, and contentment into our lives where there is none. This level of pressure in a relationship is never sustainable, and often leads to resentment, anger, and hurt. It's an expectation that can never be met. This pattern manifests in men and women who are always searching for something they feel is missing and believe that another person will magically fill their unmet needs and finally make them happy and content.

3. **Avoidance:** The third way this imbalance icing-cake pattern shows up is when people are using their relationships– or dating and the

pursuit of relationships– as a way to distract themselves from other, often uncomfortable issues in their lives. Often these people are in the midst of healing, grieving, or big learning. Instead of seeing their own internal state with clarity and engaging in the process of learning and healing, they amp up their focus on the search for the perfect relationship. On some level, they usually hold a belief that finding this person will alleviate the discomfort of their own inner process or remove their need for learning or healing altogether. This is most common when the needed learning and healing stemmed from the ending or trauma of a previous relationship.

You may recognize yourself in some of these patterns, and if you do, I would encourage you to start with self acceptance. It's completely and entirely okay to be exactly where you are, and awareness is the first step to healing. Regardless of whether you tend to lose yourself in relationships, have been hoping that the right relationship would solve all of your problems, or have been using dating to avoid your deeper work, it is never too late to begin the process of learning how to invest in your own foundational cake. It's never too late to begin to learn the importance of internal validation. It's never too late to build up your connections and resources in other areas, as long as theft are both healthy and safe, like your community, friends, and family. It's never too late to begin treating yourself like the worthy, inherently valuable, divine being that you are.

It's also important to remember that we human beings never do anything that doesn't work for us. We have this amazing part of our brain whose very existence hinges on a singular job: to keep us safe. When we have patterns like those that I've shown you in this chapter, it's never accidental or happenstance. It's never because we just woke up one day and decided to start being that way– patterns like these are always rooted in a deeper learning, specifically, a learning that occurred when something or someone else showed us that we needed to earn the love we received, or that we couldn't rely on our relationships to the expected emotional needs. For me, it was rooted in my childhood and the sense of abandonment I felt. For you, it may be something similar, or not. But the truth is, if you're ready to begin to dismantle patterns like those that stem from the icing-cake problem, you must be willing to take a clear, hard look at what you learned about love, relationships, and your own sense of self worth and value, and where you learned it. For many of us, those moments of learning occurred in our childhood, and the relationships we've had in which the pattern manifested, like my relationship with Tom, are just extensions of the original learning. And, more than that, those relationships are ultimately divine opportunities for each of us to see and dismantle the beliefs and behaviors that are not aligned with our best and highest good.

Think of it like this– you and your life are meant to be the foundation for any relationships you engage in. No other person or relationship is ever intended to be your everything. The only way to move into a place of security and wholeness in your relationships is to consciously recognize that you are okay whether you have those specific relationships or not. It isn't about not caring or a lack of effort or even that your relationships aren't important and deeply valuable– they are.

and it isn't about not needing relationships at all—you do. It's about knowing that your worth, value, and ability to be ultimately whole and okay do not depend on your relationship status with any singular person or group. No one person can provide that for you, and as long as you continue to engage in relationships without a strong inner sense of who you are, as long as you continue to put the pressure of your fulfillment on other people, the more you will experience relationships that ultimately let you down. Be in pursuit of life and of knowing yourself wholly and completely and the ultimate icing-on-the-cake love will find you, no doubt.

CREATING BETTER LOVE: BAKING

The concepts of validation, self worth, and your basic beliefs about love are elements of learning that were formed long before you ever started dating, or even thinking about relationships. As you begin to build your internal foundation, you have the opportunity to assess and intentionally shape those basic internal guidelines. Reimagining your basic beliefs about love and about yourself will help to empower you to shift your focus from looking for a relationship to fulfill you to focusing on making your cake the best it can be. The better the cake, the better the foundation for the icing, after all.

>Our goals in this process are:
>1. To evaluate our past patterns in relationships and get honest about where we have had the tendency to place unreasonable expectations on our partners.
>
>2. To consider our earliest beliefs about love, relationships, and ourselves and understand the way they are impacting our current relationships.

Get out your journal and explore the following questions. As always, resist the urge to edit or second guess your answers. Breaking the patterns that you become aware of in your relationships will require self awareness, continued understanding, deep work, and practice. It may take time to release and rewrite all of them, and that's 100% okay. Your first job is awareness, and awareness is the doorway to healing.

1. What patterns have I experienced over and over again in my relationships? Where in my relationship history have I placed the expectation of fulfillment on another person? Where has the expectiona of fulfillment been placed on me?

2. In what ways were these patterns acted out by my parents or early caregivers?

3. What did I learn about myself when it comes to love, affection, and care from my experience with my parents or early caregivers?

4. What are these patterns showing me about my relationship with myself?

5. The similarities between the care I received as a child and the patterns in my adult relationships are:

CHAPTER EIGHT
LEAVE THE PAST WHERE IT BELONGS

The story I'm about to tell you is difficult for me, but it's important. I firmly believe that all of our relationships and interactions are for us, with the greatest intention for our own learning, growth, and evolution. I do not believe that they are *about* us, in the sense that our past and our interactions are not intended to hold meaning about who we are or limit our potential, worth, or value in any way whatsoever. I cannot overemphasize how important that distinction is. So, before I share this particular piece of my past with you, let me say this: The concept of allowing our experiences to be for us and not about us is far more challenging to embrace when we are the ones that behave poorly in a relationship. The women I coach who find themselves on the receiving end of bad behavior are usually not far from ready for those interactions not to hold meaning or create limits for what is ultimately possible for them. Sometimes, however, we find ourselves in a position of being in the wrong, and part of our healing in those instances is to recognize that even decisions and behavior that we wish we could go back and change also hold insight and information for our growth. And no matter how terrible of a person you may feel like or how terrible of a decision you may believe you made, you were still never intended to be limited by your past, nor any amount of guilt or shame you may hold over what has happened.

As human beings, I genuinely believe that we are all generally doing the best we can with the resources we have. And from time to time, doing our best with what we have can mean that we hurt others or make less than stellar decisions (especially in hindsight). Your only responsibilities are to take ownership of the consequences of your behavior, apologize where needed, and move on with grace. Your responsibility ends with the commitment to raising your personal standard of "best I can" with the knowledge and insight you gained from the experience. Better love does not include hanging onto guilt for the unforeseeable future– endless, boundless guilt ultimately serves no one. If you are reading this and holding onto regret, guilt, or shame from past behaviors or decisions, no matter how recent, remember that you are human. And all humans are in deep need of grace– for ourselves and for others.

    My unhealed inner child reared her terrified, dysfunctional little head early in my twenties after I befriended Jessica and her husband at a local bar. At the time, I was feeling the pressure of a string of dates and short-lived relationships that had ended without the convenience of a clear explanation– I was feeling the full effects of the perception that I wasn't good enough. I didn't realize it then, but rejection was a huge trigger for my inner-child wounds, and experiencing it (or even the perception of experiencing it) often brought all of my latent fears and insecurities bubbling to the surface. At the time, I compensated by amping up my social life and spent a lot of time out with my new friends, usually drinking, dancing, or both. After meeting at the bar, Jess and I became fast friends– we spent nights and weekends hanging out, exchanged clothes, and went out regularly. Her husband usually tagged along.

One night, after drinking entirely too much, I found myself alone in the car with Dave, Jess' husband, while she helped another one of her friends inside the club. I was drunk, but not so drunk as to not know what was happening when Dave leaned back from the front seat, pulled down my low-cut top, and felt me up. I knew it was wrong, but I didn't protest. In fact, I didn't say anything at all. I let him do it and for that moment, instead of feeling guilty, I felt good about myself. I felt wanted.

There began a nearly four-month affair with my best friend's husband. In all fairness, we never did sleep together, but given the chance I have no doubt we would have. I let him steal kisses and feel me up whenever he had the chance. I let him text and call me every day from work, mostly to complain about his home life and Jess, the woman to whom I was supposed to be a friend. I encouraged his attraction to me. I would show up to hang out with Jess wearing outfits that he had told me to wear on the phone earlier that day. He would walk me to my car at the end of the night and kiss me or put his hand up my skirt. And I participated. I allowed it because more than anything, I wanted to be wanted, seen, and validated.

Then late one night, Jess called me in hysterics. One of her friends had seen Dave kiss me in the parking lot the last time we went out. She responded by going through his phone, and her exploration had confirmed every one of her worst fears— I, her best friend, was having an affair with her husband. Over the next few weeks, Jess spent hours on the phone with me, asking questions, crying, and berating me. At the same time, Dave left their marital home, calling me on his way out of town and begging me to go with him, claiming that he was in love with me. Thankfully, I at least had the sense to refuse.

I spent weeks and months apologizing to Jess. I explained that we hadn't slept together. I explained my teeny tiny grasp on the deep issues that I was just beginning to understand. But no manner of explaining could assuage the deep sense of betrayal I had caused within our friendship, and after the most dramatic interactions of those few weeks ended, Jess and I stopped talking altogether. In all honesty, I haven't spoken with her since.

For years after this event, I struggled with deep guilt; and in part, rightfully so. I had behaved poorly and with terrible judgment– and that's putting it mildly. There was no real way to defend my actions because they were wrong, in so many ways. There is nothing wrong with guilt in and of itself, in fact, it's a deeply important human emotion that lets us know when we've done something less than great. Guilt is an extension of our conscience and, like all emotions, is essentially neutral– it exists only to provide us with the information we need to make the next decision, and hopefully a decision that is in line with our best and highest good. Healthy guilt urges us to take responsibility for actions that were a) actually wrong and b) actually ours to take responsibility for. And healthy guilt ideally always leads to a positive decision or action.

However, guilt can become problematic when we allow it to run amok and fail to hold it to any standards. Toxic guilt comes from a damaged part of us and urges us to take responsibility for things we did not actually do or are not actually responsible for. Likewise, toxic guilt has no end— it never leads to a positive decision or behavior and it never seems to go away. We can shift healthy guilt into toxic guilt when we fail to recognize guilt for what it truly is— as a tool with a logical purpose and end.

In my case, I had done something terribly wrong for which I was responsible. The guilt that I experienced after the incident with Jess and her husband was healthy and well-placed. In response, I took every positive action that I could— I took responsibility for my role in the interaction, I refused to continue my relationship with Dave, I apologized sincerely and profusely to Jess, and I learned a very valuable lesson about just how much me and my un-managed childhood wounds could destroy things.

My guilt became problematic, however, when I found myself unable to stop living under its weight. I just couldn't let go, and my guilt ceased to be constructive. I knew I had to do something about it when my guilt began to morph into shame. To put it simply, the difference between guilt and shame is this: Guilt occurs when we believe we've done something wrong. Shame occurs when we believe that we *are* inherently wrong. Shame is an issue of self concept and self worth, and it can and will interfere with your ability to show up as your whole, complete self in any relationship. Shame will absolutely also interfere with your ability to attract an aligned relationship, because shame messes with your sense of deservedness.

The truth is, you deserve an authentic, aligned relationship experience. You deserve to find your forever person and build a beautiful life together, whatever that means to you. But, it is really difficult to tap into that sense of deservedness and the vibe it brings if you're wallowing around in shame from toxic guilt around your past. If you find yourself dealing with guilt you just can't seem to shake, or even shame around any part of your past, I encourage you to seek professional support to dismantle those feelings and where they ultimately come from. And in the meantime, here are a few tips to start the process:

1. **Assess Your Guilt**: Remember that your emotions, guilt or otherwise, exist to serve a single purpose;

emotions are neutral and only meant to provide you with more information about your inner state and your next steps. That doesn't mean that all emotions are intended to be acted upon, and that doesn't mean that all emotions are valid directional markers. It does mean that all emotions, including guilt, need to be assessed for their meaning and validity. In the case of guilt, spend some time asking yourself if the guilt you're experiencing is healthy guilt. Is your guilt urging you to take responsibility for something that is actually yours to take responsibility for? Is it coming from within you, rather than being placed on you by another person? Is it pushing you toward a positive end or a behavior, lesson, or decision that is in line with your best and highest good?

2. **Get Perspective:** Emotions like guilt, whether healthy or toxic, can be challenging because they're so deeply

personal and can hold so much meaning. Ask yourself how you would respond to a friend who was going through a similar situation. Or, better yet, ask for perspective from a trusted friend, coach, or therapist. Honest, non-judgmental feedback can be a lifesaver when it comes to sorting out your feelings of guilt and sifting the healthy from the toxic.

3. **Refocus on Growth:** Both the mistakes we make and the process of learning to evaluate our emotions are precious learning opportunities. Healthy guilt inspires positive change. Being intentional about looking for opportunities to learn and grow in the midst of your guilt can help you resolve healthy guilt and recognize when guilt has crossed into the realm of toxic, unconstructive emotions.

4. **Forgive Yourself:** Ultimately, letting go of guilt resides in forgiveness. Remember you are human and always

in a place of learning to be better. Our willingness to live in the present, have empathy for the past versions of ourselves, and learn and grow from our mistakes is part of why we're here. That ongoing process is built into your purpose. In this case, learning to cultivate unconditional love for yourself, the same way that you desire others or a future partner to love you, will serve you well.

The process of self-forgiveness and letting go of guilt over our past is one that requires time and practice. Be patient with yourself. You will likely have to repeat the practice of seeking perspective, acknowledging your learning, and releasing yourself many times. I had to work to forgive myself for my behavior with Dave and Jess. Some days, the feelings of guilt would seem to resurface out of nowhere, and I learned that my job was to acknowledge the feeling without judgment and place it into the context of what was actually true. And the truth is, we all have decisions and behaviors in our past that are less than stellar– some even downright awful. If you walk away from this book with anything, I would love for it to be freedom.

Amanda came to her first appointment with me already in tears. She had been divorced for several years, and even though she felt she was ready to explore dating and the possibility of finding another partner, she couldn't seem to get with it, in her own words. She told me that she had downloaded one of the popular apps, made a profile, and had even spent some time looking through potential profiles, she just didn't feel enthusiastic or excited about the prospect of meeting new people. She had even made several matches in the app and hadn't been able to bring herself to message anyone. This had devolved into weeks of chronic swiping that went nowhere. Amanda felt stuck.

I commended Amanda's bravery and her willingness to try something entirely new (app-based dating hadn't been a thing the last time she had dated, before her marriage) and we spent some time exploring her real readiness—sometimes, we all fall into the trap of thinking we "should" be ready to move forward or move on even when we really aren't. When we were in a place of being sure that Amanda definitely was ready and did want to start dating again, we turned to the task of finding and identifying the blocks and fears that were keeping her from moving forward.

    I asked Amanda to imagine opening her app, swiping on a person she was interested in, and sending an enthusiastic, engaging message to kick things off, and then to identify any body sensations, thoughts, or "yes, but" statements that might come up for her. For example, *"Yes, I want to start dating again, but no one will want a divorcee anyway."* Amanda closed her eyes to visualize the first steps of her new dating life, and when she opened them again, she said, "I feel guilty. But why??"

    I told her this was common and guilt could pop up anywhere in the journey– the important part was to understand it and make sure we were responding to it appropriately. I asked Amanda if she believed that starting to date again was wrong in any way. She hesitated, and then shared that she wondered if it was fair to her daughter, who had already struggled to adjust to the divorce. I nodded, and then asked her if there was anyone else in her life who might think that her beginning to date again was wrong in any way. To that, Amanda replied that she was sure her ex-husband, who did not want the divorce to happen in the first place, would very much think that she shouldn't start dating, as well as her mother, who had always criticized her for never being satisfied, including in her marriage. As we dig deeper into the three sources of Amanda's guilt around dating, I challenged her to identify the roots of those feelings and to assess whether the guilt she was experiencing was healthy and pushing her toward positive action, or whether it was unhealthy and keeping her stuck.

As we unpacked the guilt Amanda was experiencing, she started to identify some deeper core issues. Namely, the criticism from her mother had caused part of her to believe that she was broken in some way– she spent much of her childhood and adolescence believing that there must be something wrong with her because she wasn't ever satisfied, which caused her to second guess her own feelings and desires even as an adult. The truth was, Amanda's mother had herself settled in an abusive relationship with an alcoholic, and was likely triggered by Amanda's ability to move on from circumstances and situations that didn't feel aligned for her. What

Amanda was experiencing as a result of chronic criticism was shame, not guilt, and it had kept her in a place of second-guessing herself– both her divorce and now her decision to start dating again. I explained to Amanda that her decision to divorce her husband was her own, and that his not wanting the divorce himself could feel like it added an extra layer of difficulty to the situation. Specifically, having opposition so close to home challenged Amanda's resolution when it came to her own decision, just like her mother's criticism had for most of her life.

    I led Amanda through an exercise designed to help her release the impact her mother's criticism had on her by shifting her perspective around how 'correct' her mother's feedback had been. As a child, she had understandably been unable to see that her mother's criticism had nothing to do with her and everything to do with her mother herself, but her adult self could. She could create a grown up resource state to refer back to when that version of her inner child was triggered. By the end of the session, Amanda recognized that the guilt she was feeling about dating and her divorce from her mother and her ex husband was not healthy guilt– it had been a mix of shame and unhealthy guilt that was keeping her stuck.

    We then explored Amanda's sense of guilt around her daughter and the impact she was imagining starting to date might have on her after the transition of the divorce. I encouraged Amanda to use that feeling to make a positive step in her relationship with her daughter. Since Amanda's daughter was a teenager and it was age-appropriate, I asked her if she would consider having a conversation with her daughter about how she was feeling about the divorce and the changes that had occurred for both of them over the last few years, and then to share with her daughter the sense of guilt she was carrying about taking the next steps in her personal life by exploring dating. That way, she was acknowledging the feeling at hand instead of using it to create a narrative that may or may not have been true and creating space to explore whether her concerns were founded. I also reminded her that doing so would mean she was modeling healthy communication to her daughter and taking a step toward interrupting the cycle of dysfunction she had inherited from her own mother.

Amanda did have that conversation with her daughter – several, in fact. She returned to our next session feeling good about how they had connected and communicated. Her daughter assured Amanda that she wanted her to be happy, and finding a new relationship was part of that. They worked over the next few months to establish some ground rules that kept them both feeling comfortable moving forward, and also addressing some needs her daughter expressed as having stemmed from the divorce. I reminded Amanda that the guilt she was feeling about dating when it came to her daughter was no longer necessary. Their communication had alleviated any need for it to be present, and she could healthily let it go. It served its purpose of inspiring reconciliation and positive action. We were able to move onto exploring how to navigate the apps more effectively and how to help Amanda start those conversations she had been previously avoiding. She no longer felt guilt around wanting to date, and aside from some jitters related to inexperience, Amanda didn't feel any negative feelings when she imagined, or practiced, engaging in the process of dating anymore.

Here's the takeaway: You are not limited by your past. Whatever mistakes and bad decisions you made or shitty relationships you've endured, your future life in love is not limited by what has come before. Leave what is in the past, in the past. It is all intended for your learning and your growth, and there is only forward from here on out. It is so easy to fall into the oh-so-human trap of believing we aren't worthy of the best and brightest version of our future, but as easy as it may seem, that belief is never true.

Onward and upward, love. If you've been holding onto the past as a means to keep yourself from the future, it's time to begin the process of letting it go. You deserve nothing less than to leave your past exactly where it belongs. New ways of being, new patterns, new realizations, and new relationships are always available to you. And, most importantly, it's all available to you regardless of what your past contains. Your pursuit of better love will require you to unlatch yourself from what came before and recognize that it only represents your path of learning and growth, nothing more. Your future lies ahead of you, wide and bright and filled with love, just waiting for you to claim it. Let the past be the past and take your first step forward right now.

CREATING BETTER LOVE: RELEASE THE PAST

Part of doing big, heart-healing work is to be in the practice of putting the past into context with what is actually true. For example, I could have spent the rest of my life feeling guilty about what I did to Jess and Dave, but the truth is, once I took responsibility for my actions and committed to learning from them and doing better in the future, guilt served no purpose in that situation. It certainly didn't align with my best and brightest future nor my greatest and highest good. Use the following prompts and some time with your favorite journal to explore your own past and the things you might be holding onto that could be keeping you from embracing your future.

Our goals in this process are:
1. To begin to explore our past from the perspective of what is actually true and consider putting those experiences that were challenging into a perspective that is

fully future oriented.

2. To identify the parts of our past that we are unnecessarily holding onto and need to release, and the parts of our past for which we need to take responsibility.

3. To free ourselves from any toxic guilt we may be holding and recognize the places we may be using our past to keep ourselves from the future we deserve.

Get out your journal and explore the following questions. Resist the urge to edit or second-guess your answers. There's no need to judge yourself or whatever happened before. Whatever comes to mind is exactly what's intended to come up for you right now. And remember, guilt, especially toxic guilt, isn't always rational. You may need professional support to move through your past experiences and cultivate forgiveness for yourself, and if that's the case for you, that's entirely okay. Give yourself permission to seek out any help or support you may need.

1. Consider your past relationships— both romantic and not— and ask yourself where

you may be feeling guilt or shame around any circumstances of the past. Consider behavior in the relationships, how things ended, or things you said, did, or expected that you know better than to do now.

2. Imagine that any guilt you may be carrying had a voice – in fact, go ahead and create a caricature of your guilt. What does it look like? What would it say to you? How does it make you feel? Is it constructive or damaging?

3. What areas may you need to take responsibility for your choices or your actions? How does taking responsibility in this case need to look – is it for you, or are other people involved?

4. What areas may you be holding onto toxic guilt? Does it belong to someone else, or have you placed it on yourself? How do you know it's toxic?

5. What would it feel like to consider forgiving yourself for your past today? What would

you need to be able to release yourself from the past once and for all?

There are no shortcuts when it comes to evaluating and ultimately releasing ourselves from our pasts– it is, above all else, a process. Know that no matter where you are on the path of releasing guilt, you are absolutely and unquestionably deserving of grace and freedom just as you are in this moment. You are loved– always– and no amount of baggage or bad behavior can override that basic, human truth.

– CHAPTER NINE –
FEEL YOUR WAY

I always loved Oliva Newton John's transformation at the end of the movie *Grease*. Not only did she look like absolute *fire* in those spandex pants and red heels, but the back and forth of not knowing who she was, what she wanted, or if she was even permitted to have what she thought she wanted in the first place seemed to dissipate with her perm and outfit change. I remember watching that movie as an awkward preteen and longing for her ability to demand nothing less than exactly what she desired. Long after the first time I saw the movie, I realized that going for exactly what I wanted was an important part of creating the relationships I wanted to have in my life. In my experience, most of us spend far too much time and energy pursuing relationships we already know aren't actually what we want. Perhaps we find ourselves settling for something we would have deemed a 'deal breaker' before, or perhaps we realize there is some fundamental quality missing from the relationship in question. Or maybe we've convinced ourselves that we can fix whatever is wrong with the relationship or the other person, hanging our hat on pure potential. Ultimately, it's fear that keeps us in these situations. Namely, the fear that there's nothing more available to us, fear of being alone, or fear of being rejected.

    In my years of personal healing and in my years of working with women from all over the world, I know this: The longer you settle for saying 'yes' to the things you do not want, the longer you are keeping yourself from finding the things you do want. More importantly, the longer you accept things in your relationships that are not in line with what you ultimately want to create, the longer you are telling yourself and others that it's okay to accept less-than and that what you really, truly desire isn't that important after all. The biggest obstacle I encounter when coaching women on dating to find their aligned relationship is that most people don't take the time and energy to consider why they're dating in the first place. It seems so simple, but most of us spend more time waiting to be chosen, wondering if we're good enough for whoever is showing us attention in the moment, or planning Pinterest weddings to hypothetical partners to ever stop and answer the question, "What exactly do I want?"

In the full swing of healing my dating patterns, I realized that I needed to get really clear about what I was looking for. After all, how could I practice consciousness, boundaries, expansiveness, and all the other mindset shifts I was learning if I didn't know what my end goal was? How could I say no to what wasn't aligned if I didn't invest time into figuring out what *was* aligned? If you– and I– want to do anything better, it should be done intentionally and with a goal, and dating is no exception.

Admittedly, most of us don't associate dating with goals and intentions. When we think about dating, we think about the experience first. We dream of spontaneously finding the one, being swept off our feet, whisked away from our normal lives in a feel-good cloud of flowers, chocolate hearts, and killer orgasms. When I ask clients to associate goals and intentions with dating, it can feel like it takes some of the magic out of the process. But truly, the magic is still very much there. I'm just asking you to take advantage of the amazing opportunity to get clear on how the magic is going to show up in your life. I'll say it again and again— **there is power in clarity.**

You might be wondering why prince charming can't just spontaneously show up and whisk you away to happily ever after. And, believe me, I get it. I used to think that just being a person in the world meant love would work for me, regardless of how many times it hadn't. I believed that I could just go about my business while my forever-love was being divinely orchestrated on my behalf, and when that didn't work, I resorted to anything I could think of to 'fix myself' into being more desirable and more acceptable. It never occurred to me then that my aimless man hunting wasn't serving me— I thought I was holding out for the ultimate romance. But the truth is, dating with clear goals is important for a number of reasons.

First, goals provide us with direction. The exercise of getting clear about what we want to create and committing to that vision forces us to keep the direction we're headed and the outcome we're after at the forefront of our minds. It helps prevent us from mindlessly repeating the same patterns, relationships, and habits over and over again. Having clear goals in dating also offers us a more tangible path to make decisions about next steps with ease. Paths have boundaries, clearly defined edges to guide you through space. Our awareness of those boundaries helps us make choices that keep us on the path, rather than bumbling off of it.

If you're clear about what you're creating and what you desire out of the dating process, your clarity will act as a guide as you move forward. Dating without direction is like wandering a maze, never knowing when the next dead-end will stop you in your tracks. Dating with clear goals and intentions in mind is more like driving along a highway– sure, you may get off an exit or two along the way, but the direction is always clearly marked and getting back on track is easy. It comes down to this: **Making decisions that are in line with your ultimate desires is easier when you know what your desires are.**

    It seems so simple, doesn't it? But I still struggled, and I've worked with many others who have as well. Thankfully, after years of coaching, I've pared down the art of dating with clarity and intention to two, very manageable processes. They will seem simple, but they work. They work because they require your commitment and offer you an easy way to keep your purpose and direction in mind, no matter what kind of date you end up on. They work because they're attainable, practical steps that will bring you closer to clarity and get you in touch with what you really want. The first step? Make a list.

    I know, *I know*– you've probably seen coach after coach tell you to make a list to attract your soul mate. And for as many coaches who tell you writing a list is a great idea, there are just as many who condemn it as a trite practice in futility. But to be clear– I can assure you that there is great value in the practice of creating your list, but it may not be for the reasons that you think. See, the list you create isn't for the universe. God doesn't need your shopping list for the perfect partner, but *you do.*

There is no magic in the list itself– the list is a practical tool to keep you connected and aware of what you want as you wade through the dating pool and everything it can bring your way. If a date goes horribly wrong, it's usually easier to recognize that you may not want to pursue a connection with that person. It can be more difficult, however, when your date isn't so bad, or, perhaps, it's actually pretty great. Not everyone you meet is meant for you, and not every person that isn't meant for you will be obvious about it. When I ended my date with AJ (remember the Hallmark cards?) by calling the police, I obviously knew that guy wasn't for me. But later, when I met an impeccably polite lawyer who was also an accomplished fine artist for coffee in my favorite part of the city, it was a little more difficult to recognize that he and I weren't a good match. This is where your list comes in.

Your list is intended to act as a collection of guidelines to keep you moving forward and on track with creating your best relationships. It helps you focus and stay in alignment with what you want to create in your love life as you engage in the process of dating. Your list answers the questions: What is your end goal when it comes to dating? Why are you doing it? What are you hoping to manifest and create in your love life? What kind of relationship are you looking for? How do you want to feel in your ideal relationship? What does your ideal relationship look like? How would you know if it were right in front of you?

When you're ready to craft your ultimate list, here are a few of my best guidelines to help you make it the powerful tool that it can be:

1. **Edit your list as often as you feel led.** You aren't married to the first version of your list, or even the hundredth. Part of the purpose of the list is to change and evolve as you grow and learn. Remember, dating is a process and your relationships are always in the business of teaching you more about yourself. What you

desire in a relationship will most definitely change as you engage in the process, because in the process of dating and engaging in relationships will most definitely change you.

2. **Focus on feelings.** Avoid the temptation to make your list into a grocery list of hyper-specific attributes of another person. Your list is for you, and it should focus on quality-based content about your ideal relationship and ideal partner. Focus on how you want to feel in your ideal relationship, shared values you would love to have with your ideal partner, and passions and experiences that are important to you. It is far more useful to be concerned with how your partner will show love than whether he's over 6' or 5'11". Compatibility is far more lasting and important than physical chemistry alone.

3. **No judgment.** The things you desire in your future ideal relationship are yours to desire, no judgment required. Whether you deeply desire someone who can financially support you, dream of being a stay at home mom or want a partner who will stay at home with your brood, would love a person as obsessed with travel as you are, or even someone to be madly in love with but keep separate apartments, your desires are intentional. Your desires hold value and meaning for you. You don't need to second guess your list based on any perception of what's okay or what isn't outside of your own self and your own feelings.

4. **Desires Only.** Keep the list focused on what you do want, and don't include any items or descriptions of what you don't want. You're investing time and energy into really identifying what's important to you. Focusing on what you don't want, or even what

you've had in the past that didn't work isn't an effective use of your energy in this case. After all, you don't go to your local coffee shop and tell the barista everything on the menu you're not interested in ordering, you identify what you do want in order to receive it.

5. **Write in the Present Tense.** Instead of sticking your love list out in the undetermined future, write it as if it's already here. So, instead of writing, "I want to feel like a priority", write "I am a priority." You are creating your future by calling it into your reality as you create it. Writing in the present tense helps you really tune into the feelings and the possibility of what's available to you.

6. **Revisit Your List.** Do not, and I repeat, do not write your list and then stick it in a drawer or notebook and ignore it. The list is for you to

use as a tool while you date. It serves as a reminder of what you're looking for and what you desire to create in your love life. It will help you in your practice of alignment. It will make recognizing potential partners and dates that aren't aligned with what you're looking for easier to spot sooner. Ultimately, committing to working your list can help prevent you from falling into the trap of over-involving with a guy you *think* is the one, only to be disappointed and surprised later by all the red flags you missed or ignored.

Once you have your list in hand, the second part of your intentional, purpose-driven dating process is to practice without attachment. Specifically, you're meant to show up and allow dating to be the process that it was meant to be, all while being guided by your list but not attached to it. Treating your list as a set of guidelines intended to grow and evolve empowers you to find ongoing clarity while you date. Attachment, on the other hand, is the need for a specific outcome, in this case the exact contents of your list in the exact way you imagined them, to make you happy. 'Need' is a very different vibration than 'have'— there is no faith in desperation. Your goal when it comes to your list is to be in the place of wanting while looking forward to receiving, and enjoying every moment in between. Attachment to your list overrides the freedom and learning in your dating experience. Attachment stems from fear, desperation, and inflexibility— a lack of faith that your aligned match is really a possibility for you.

      Dating is designed to act as a path— a funnel, remember? The funnel of dating is moving you along through your interactions, relationships, and lessons, inviting you all the while to learn, grow, and evolve— and have fun along the way. Not every person you meet will align with your list, nor are they meant to. These relationships are like stepping stones along your path, and while each person you end up on a date with may not be a representation of your list, they still hold value for you. As you date, you are collecting data about yourself, about others, about what you do and do not want in relationships– everything you experience is more information. In dating, this is why it can be problematic to fall into a pattern of blaming and bitterness whenever a potential relationship doesn't work out the way you imagined it would. This is where the practice of neutrality becomes king (or queen).

When we learn to experience dating as a process of learning, experiencing, and gathering data from which we can ultimately learn and then use to make more aligned choices moving forward, we no longer need to figure out who was at fault or what might be wrong with us whenever we add another 'no, not this one' to our list of past relationships. Will the dating process be difficult at times? Yes! Will the ending of relationships sometimes hurt? Yes! Will you have to grieve some relationships longer than others, and will you need to continue to heal as you move along the path? A resounding yes. You are human, after all. But moving forward is much easier from the perspective of dating with purpose. It is much more empowering to know that my past failed relationships served a greater purpose and were ultimately leading me along a path of learning and growing into a relationship that was right for me, rather than holding onto hurt, anger, and bitterness from each relationship that didn't work. Or worse, thinking my past failed relationships meant there was something wrong with me.

When I learned to be intentional about what I wanted from a relationship and to practice dating from a place of clarity, and when I dropped my attachment to the outcome every time I met a new person, the types of relationships I attracted changed. I started to be able to see learning opportunities as they happened, rather than years later in retrospect. I began to see the evolution of my potential partners as my dating life aligned with what I was intentionally manifesting into my experience. I gained confidence as I began dating with anticipation and holding positive expectations for what each new connection could add to my experience.

The very first date I agreed to when I first began my intentional dating journey was with a guy named Matt. We connected on one of the big-name dating sites at the time and hit it off right away. Matt was a very cool musician who collected vinyl records and was going to school for illustration. At the time, I couldn't believe that I had found someone I was so interested in so quickly; in fact, it never occurred to me that I would be so excited to meet my very first match. We set up a time to meet at a popular bar in the city, and all I remember about getting ready that night was how much overwhelming anticipation I felt. You know- the "change outfits at least ten times and question all of your life choices" kind of anticipation.

    My drive into the city was riddled with questions of disbelief- how could a guy this cool and interesting actually be interested in me?- and a lot of rehearsing introductions and hypothetical conversations in which I was perfectly witty and perfectly endearing (out loud, of course. You know you do it too!). By the time I was parking my car, I was nervous enough to puke, and twenty minutes later, I was standing across the street from the bar in question watching the guy I recognized as Matt lean against the building smoking a cigarette. He had been attractive in his profile pictures, but in person, he was downright gorgeous. I stood there watching him for at least ten minutes. He was smiling and chatting with people as they walked by and running his hand through perfectly tousled dirty blonde hair between drags. Everything about him seemed easy and effortless. And did I mention how hot he was?

The longer I stood there watching Matt basically embody effortless cool and smoldering desire on the street corner, the more anxiety I felt about whether or not I was good enough for a guy like him. I silently picked apart my outfit, my body, my attractiveness, my social skills, and anything else I could grab onto that I perceived as being flawed. And sadly, in the midst of my self-destructive spiral toward an all out panic attack, I decided that Matt was too good for me. There was no way this date wouldn't lead to rejection. I left without ever meeting him.

I spent a week feeling bad about myself and guilty for ghosting someone, all while justifying my choices with the belief that he would have rejected me anyway. I told myself that I was just saving us both the time and the trouble. The following weekend, I recounted my story to a good friend. When I got to the part about running back to my car to leave before the date even had the chance to begin, she looked at me and said, "Who are you to decide what he's interested in?" Honestly, I had expected her to be comforting and kind. I expected her to tell me I was great and reassure me that I was actually pretty enough– instead, she dropped a big fat dating lesson right into my lap. And she wasn't wrong! If I stepped outside of my own insecurity, the truth was, I had no way of knowing whether Matt would have rejected me or not. I had no actual way of knowing what Matt was interested in or attracted to at all, and for all I actually knew, he could have been head over heels into me. My response to Matt wasn't really about Matt, no matter how physically attractive he may have been; my response to Matt was a very clear reflection of how I felt about myself. I had some self-esteem and self worth issues to heal, and thanks to ultra-hot Matt, I knew exactly what I needed to focus on next.

    I didn't quite realize it at that moment, but Matt was my first step to actually practicing and applying the concept of intentional dating. And as I continued along that path, I was called again and again to commit to healing the issues and patterns that were shown to me through the mirrors of my relationships. I learned that the intentional practice of dating wasn't just about finding relationships that were more and more aligned with what I was looking for, but that it was also about me learning to embody a person that was capable of showing up in that ultimate, aligned relationship I was dreaming of. The truth is, if I had attracted my perfect partner at the same moment I had met Matt, I would not have been able to sustain that relationship. I was not yet standing in the full expression of myself. I was still wounded, limited, and desperately in need of self-awareness and healing.

I've helped many women make their own lists over the years. I've noticed that even the act of making the list can bring up opportunities to heal. This was never more clear than in one of the cohorts of my Love without Limits group coaching program. I run this limited-time group several times a year, and in this particular round, we took on the list making exercise as a way to prepare for the group to end and to empower the women in the group to step out into their actual lives in a way that was empowering and reflected all of the healing work that had done over the 8 weeks we spent together. I thought that after all the tough, emotional work they had already done, the list exercise would be fairly easy for them.

I was wrong.

As each of the women worked on their list, a myriad of triggers and issues surfaced. Several realized that they had never stopped to ask themselves what they wanted, and instead had spent a lifetime sacrificing their own desires for acceptance from others and scraps of love in underwhelming relationships. They had to process the grief that came up around those past connections and all of the feelings of sadness, anger, and hurt they felt when they recognized that pattern in real time. Other women struggled with deep issues of deservedness. They couldn't bring themselves to be honest about what they wanted in their ideal partnership because doing so made them feel so inadequate. One woman said, "What's the point of writing it down if it isn't possible anyway?" Another woman, on the opposite end of that spectrum, found herself so inflexibly wrapped up in hyper-specific requirements that didn't really do a good job of describing a relational experience as much as they painted a very specific picture of someone who was essentially George Clooney, but a little taller.

  This is normal. Expect it. As you dig into your own love list, and even more so when you begin practicing and applying it in your life, it will likely bring awareness to standing issues that need to be addressed or even trigger big emotions, memories, or beliefs that are no longer serving you. And while all of those issues look different on the surface, most of them are rooted in self-protection. Whether it's standards that are too loose, standards that are impossibly high, a sense that you don't deserve what you desire, or even a belief that it isn't possible to have it anyway, we are all just trying to protect ourselves from pain, rejection, and disappointment. Your list is an invitation to begin to heal those fears in yourself. There is nothing wrong with wanting to protect yourself– it is perfectly natural and human– but consider this an invitation to begin considering that there are better ways to protect yourself than by sacrificing your needs, desires, and standards.

  The list that you create and the process you commit to in dating is 100% about you and your healing. These days, I'm grateful for hot-guy Matt and the lessons he triggered in my own life, even if we never met. Your relationships, whether they be singular dates, long term situationships, or even your relationship with your ideal partner, are intended for your growth and evolution. They are intended to teach you more about yourself. As you learn and grow, your list will change. As you recognize your true, inherent worth and value, your list will change. As you embody more of your true self, your list will change. Don't fall into the trap of attaching yourself to your list in any one of its many incarnations- it's all a process and it all hinges on your commitment to participating and your willingness to learn.

I did end up meeting the man who embodied my list, and by the time I got to that point in my own healing journey, it wasn't difficult to recognize that he was the person I wanted to settle down with. There was no confusion, no questioning, and when I chose him, I knew I was actually choosing myself.

CREATING BETTER LOVE: THE LIST

What better way to end this chapter than to begin your own Love List? Even if you've written lists before, I'd encourage you to view this as a chance to put energy into a new beginning. Give yourself permission to create this version of your list free and clear from your past and anything that has come before. And remember, there is no magic in this list– Prince Charming won't come barging in your door moments after you've written a list of what you're looking for in a relationship, but your list will serve as a starting point for your to embark on the process of dating with intention, clarity, and purpose.

Our goals in this process are:
1. To begin to explore what we actually desire to experience and create in our relationships, and to understand our goals when it comes to dating.

2. To create a living, breathing guideline for future dating, meant to help us recognize when interactions with others are aligned with us and when they aren't.

3. To create a resource that supports the perspective of dating with intention and purpose and helps us engage in our own healing and growth.

Get out your journal and explore the following questions. Resist the urge to edit or second guess your answers. There's no need to judge yourself or your past. Whatever comes to mind is exactly what's intended to come up for you at this moment. Use this as a divine opportunity to explore whatever your soul desires. Refer back to the guidelines in this chapter as needed!

1. How do you want to feel in your ideal relationship?

2. How would you know your ideal relationship is 'the one'?

3. What values do you want your ideal partner to share with you?

4. What experiences, hobbies, or lifestyle is important to you in your ideal relationship?

5. How do you want your ideal partner to show you love?

6. Imagine an ideal date with your partner, what do you do? How do you feel? What

makes it perfect?

7. What elements of past relationships really worked for you? What are you grateful for when it comes to your past relationships?

Use all of the ideas, inspirations, and answers that came to you as you explored the above questions to compile the first version of your Love List. Remember to write in the present tense and to focus on the feelings and quality of the relationship you're attracting. You can begin to use your list as guidance right away, starting with considering bringing closure to any lingering or current relationships that are not in alignment with what you want to create in your life.

– CHAPTER TEN –
LEARN YOUR LOVE SUBSTITUTES

Finding love, settling down with a partner, and creating your very own version of a family can feel like an inevitable milestone, like learning to walk, going to school, or getting your first job. So much so that we spend an inordinate time of money, resources, time, and energy pursuing the perfect partner. We have apps, websites, books, coaches, meetups, singles events, and more. In fact, it's estimated that in 2020, the online dating industry alone boasted a market worth over 3 billion dollars.

We are a society obsessed with finding love. And, truthfully, there's a reason for that. This chapter will ultimately be about being single, but let me start with this: It is completely normal, honorable, and beautiful that you desire love and a partnership that is truly aligned with who you are. That desire was given to you for a reason, and it is my firm belief that we are not given desires in this life that we aren't meant to have. Human beings are not created to be alone, not to be 100% independent of others. Our problem, as humans living in a world of lessons and hardships and imbalance, are all the misguided ways we often try to fulfill those desires.

You have been created for this– you are biologically, psychologically, and spiritually designed to desire and seek out love, partnership, care, support, intimacy, and relationships. Don't ever let anyone tell you that there's anything wrong with wanting love.

In fact, the survival of your very early ancestors depended on it. Intimate, dynamic interactions supported reproduction, growth, and mutual benefits necessary for survival. When you see a person you are romantically connected to, or interested in, specific areas of your brain are activated– different areas that we see activated by other forms of connection, like that between a mother and a child or siblings. At the same time, the areas of the brain associated with negative emotions, criticism, and social judgment are deactivated, allowing us to be more open to forming a bond with the object of our interest. Researchers have also found that the experience of falling in love and being attracted to potential partners activates the parts of the brain associated with reward and motivation.

In other words, your brain is actively encouraging you toward love. Your desire to connect is natural, biological, and powerful.

Let's go back to the bit about how we as humans can make the mistake of trying to fulfill our completely valid desires in all the wrong ways. This is a problem that manifests so easily when it comes to romantic connections. How many of us have taken our valid, natural drive to develop romantic bonds and intimate connections and tried to meet that need with misaligned relationships, one-night stands, staying in partnerships that weren't good for us, food, alcohol, partying, or... fill in the blank with your own personal love-substitute.

Love-substitutes are the things we use to fill our inherent need for love, intimacy, and connection that aren't actually that at all. These substitutions usually help us feel connected, cared for, or seen for a short period of time, while also enabling us to avoid the deeper issues and hard questions surrounding the lack of love in our experience. Much like artificial sweeteners, they leave us wanting more and usually have a weird aftertaste.

The challenge of our substitutions usually stems from denial. Often, we are so driven by our need for intimacy and connection that we fail to see the places in our lives where we have been accepting less than the real-deal. We deny the fact that we're running on the drive of unmet emotional needs and classify our fill-the-void behaviors as standard. Sometimes, we don't even genuinely like these coping mechanisms, we just haven't learned a better way to respond to our innate need to connect.

The key when it comes to love-substitutes is both to contextualize our desire for love and connection as real and valid, but also to recognize what our own love-substitutes tend to be. And, like many things, the place to start is usually in hindsight.

My own love-substitutes hit hard in my early dating life, and they all revolved around one primary need: validation.

For a period of time, I hooked my self worth and my sense of value to whoever was showing me enough attention to make me feel validated. In practice, this took the form of going home with men I didn't know and wouldn't have been interested in in normal circumstances, friends with benefits, wasting my time with men who didn't want a relationship but wanted all the benefits of a relationship, and allowing myself to be undervalued and disrespected in exchange for short-lived moments that felt like intimacy.

I rationalized all of this as a part of the dating process. I called it "'living my best single life", "playing the field", and "having fun". I thought I was effectively bucking a super strict upbringing and finally stepping out, but in reality, I was living to the standards of the same trauma that made me, I had just flipped it around and applied it to my love life.

In my personal journey and my work with hundreds of other women, I've found that our love substitutes are often based on coping mechanisms we learn as children and teenagers; this is the time when we're learning how to "be" in the world and interact with other humans. One of the biggest lessons we learn in our youth is an understanding of how love works. Not romantic love, per se, but love nonetheless; the kind of love that is basic to all human survival– love rooted in security, care, and protection. We are born in absolute need of our caretakers, and we depend on our basic needs being met by others, both physical and emotional. Because many of these needs are nonnegotiable and rooted in our biology, we learn very quickly how to navigate them in an effort to get what we need. And because children aren't born with the emotional maturity to contextualize the experiences they have or the things they observe growing up, it isn't difficult for us to turn those things into truths that may not actually be entirely accurate.

In this way, we apply the lessons we learn from our earliest caretakers to our grown up romantic relationships, and we transfer the mechanisms we used to try to ensure our childhood needs would be met to our adult love-substitutes.

You may not remember all of your own developmental experiences when it comes to love and security, but you likely remember some of them, especially if they were significant. I have a vivid memory from when I was about five years old. I was sitting in the living room in the home that I grew up in, eating cereal and watching a popular children's show with my sister when my dad walked out carrying two suitcases. I remember the suitcases more than I remember anything else– they were brown tweed with a fake, orange-hued leather trim. My mom followed him out in a robe, her wet hair wrapped up in a towel. I don't remember them speaking, but I jumped up from my spot on the carpet and followed my dad to the door. Like any five year old, I had a million and a half questions– "Where are you going? When will you be back? Daddy, why are you leaving? Can I come with you?"

    My dad didn't respond to any of my questions, and I probably didn't think twice at the time, but this was one of the first moments in my life where I unwittingly learned the false belief that my experience, my feelings, and ultimately myself were not important. The more time passed that I didn't see my dad, the more distressed I became by his absence. In my little, developing mind, I believed that the relationships, or lack thereof, I had with my caretakers reflected on me and my worth. The belief that I wasn't important eventually morphed into "I'm not enough." Specifically I wasn't enough for my dad to stay, to choose to pursue or maintain a relationship with me, or to fight for my sister and I. In all actuality, I had no way of knowing the adult conflicts, dilemmas, and efforts either of my parents encountered on my behalf, but our perception of reality is what informs the meaning we apply to our experiences. It's our perception of the truth that eventually informs our behavior.

An internalized belief that I wasn't enough for love, care, or effort meant that my unconscious mind would naturally drive me to remedy that unmet need in whatever way felt most accessible– it was a hunt for the validation of my own worth and value. I learned that I could get validation from the adults around me by being good. Perfect grades were met with positive attention and affirmation that the people around me loved me and were proud of me. The same for agreeable behavior, awards and accolades, and sacrificing my own interests for what I believed people wanted from me.

As a child, it seemed harmless enough– I was a straight 'A' student, teachers and adults always thought highly of me, and I never caused any trouble. On the surface, there's nothing wrong with those things. The problem was my motivation— I did those things because I believed that they made me worthy of being loved.

My personal brand of love-substitute is how I ended up practically shoving a long-time, very-much-not-single friend, clutching his shoes and shirt, out of the back door of my house as my soon-to-be ex parked in the front.

Jack had been a good friend for years and we hung out, flirted, and drank together often; the night before had been no exception. He was technically off-limits, but our relationship was comfortable and I absolutely adored the attention he gave me.

It was affirming, and being around him made me feel important, valuable, and seen, even if it was always short lived.

That particular night, the alcohol flowed freely (just having fun, right?). Jack's normal flirting had turned physical, and I was all about it. In my mind, more intimacy equated to more validation. If Jack wanted me, then it confirmed that I was desirable, and desirable meant valuable. I rode that train as far as it would take me, which in this case was back to my house and into my bed.

The next morning, as I was just waking up and discovering just how hungover I was, my phone lit up signaling a text.

It was my fiance, who had not technically broken up with me, but had suggested we take a break a few weeks earlier. He was coming back to our shared apartment to talk and get some of his things– and that meant I didn't have much time.

I shook Jack awake. In the middle of his adorable grin and him asking to take me to breakfast, I was shoving clothes and shoes into his arms. "The man I am still technically, sort of engaged to will be here in 10 minutes and neither of us wants to deal with that."

That got Jack up and out of bed, throwing on clothes and socks as he went. When we made it downstairs, I could see we were already out of time. I shoved Jack out of the back sliding doors, shoeless and shirtless, just as my current situation was walking through the front door.

The conversation we ended up having was the official breakup conversation.

You already know the gist of it if you read the previous chapters. He didn't love me anymore, maybe never had, wasn't happy in our relationship, and so on. I begged, cried, and bargained with him to stay. I promised him the world. When that didn't work, I seduced him and slept with him in the same bed I had hustled Jack out of an hour earlier.

And as we lay there afterward, I looked at him, hoping that he would tell me he loved me again. Believing that it was possible that I had changed his mind about me and that I had proven I was worth loving.

Instead, he got up, went to the bathroom, and started packing his things.

He left thirty minutes later, and I was still begging him not to go.

I would reflect on that moment many times over my own healing journey; the marked similarities between that moment and the day my dad left, how I had essentially used my sacred-self to search for any semblance of worth with two different men in the span of less than six hours. It didn't feel like a proud moment, and yet, I hadn't thought twice when it was happening.

I was searching for a validation fix. I was trying to use sex, intimacy, and any connection I could garner to meet a very basic human need without fully understanding that intimacy should be earned and validation wasn't supposed to come from flash-in-the-pan moments void of meaning and depth.

I knew Jack wasn't truly available to me and had no interest in pursuing a relationship with me outside of casual, drunken sex when it was convenient. I knew that my relationship with my fiance had already met its inevitable end. And, part of me even knew that sleeping with him wouldn't ultimately change anything, even if he had happened to change his mind at that moment– the issues ran too long and too deep.

These behaviors had become my love-substitutes. I was using them to fill my natural need for love. It would take me years to realize that by indulging in love-substitute behaviors, I was just avoiding doing the necessary, deeper healing work that would eventually lead me to finding real love. Most importantly, they were keeping me from the divine realization that the source of my inherent worth and value was never and had never been seated outside of myself.

The most important thing you need to understand about love-substitutes may surprise you– *They work.* Humans don't do things that don't feel like they accomplish what we want them to accomplish in the moment– and if you're subconscious mind is desperately trying to recreate feelings of acceptance, love, validation, and worth, it will choose the things that seem to solve the problem in the most accessible, fastest ways.

And yet, the real truth is, they don't actually solve the bigger problem or meet the ultimate need. No matter how accessible or fast they may be, they never truly meet the long term need that they're intended to meet. They can never replace the work to heal and the experience of the real thing. They are cheap replacements, coping mechanisms, delay tactics– and they are keeping you from claiming true love.

Love-substitutes can look like:
- Approval-seeking behavior
- People pleasing
- Staying in or pursuing relationships long after they've expired
- Compromising standards or tolerating manipulation or abuse for intermittent positive moments of love or validation
- Chasing unavailable partners

- Engaging in on-again off-again connections because the drama is addicting (it offers just enough positive experience that you make excuses for it, or you struggle to let go)
- Compromising your own boundaries for the approval of others
- Using sex as a source of validation
- Avoiding intimate relationships and using food, shopping, alcohol, or drugs to self-soothe
- Chronic swiping, dating, or searching because nothing ever feels right or good enough

All of these behaviors will sabotage your dating life in real time. They'll make it difficult to choose partners who will authentically connect with you and make unsustainable connections way more appealing than they should be. Left unaddressed, they will cause you to undermine relationships with genuinely good potential. Simply put, using love substitutes as a quick fix to meet that need, whatever it may be for you, will prevent you from recognizing real love, even if it's staring you in the face.

The first step to healing is to recognize what experiences or behaviors you are or have been using to help you fill your basic emotional needs for love, acceptance, validation, and intimacy, especially when true love and acceptance felt unavailable for you.

The second step is connecting that unmet need to its root. Most likely, it didn't start now, and it probably didn't even begin recently. Your subconscious mind has learned to cope with the experience that something necessary to your wellbeing and safety was missing. This begins with a series of deceptively simple questions:

1. What's the basic need your love-substitutes are designed to meet?
2. When was the first time (or earliest memory you have) that you learned the answer to that basic need wasn't readily available to you or wouldn't be met?
3. How do your love-substitutes help you feel more of what you experienced as missing? In what ways do they work?
4. What is the truth about that core need? Where is its true source?

In order to have any revelation about my own love-substitutes, I first had to recognize why I had created them in the first place. I had to recognize that the core need my brain experienced as missing was validation. Yours may be different, but as a child, I wanted nothing more than for my caretakers to validate that I was important, valuable, and a priority. The more I dug, the more stories I unearthed that represented moments that I received or perceived a message that I wasn't important.

Psychologically, it is nearly impossible for children to adequately assign responsibility to their caretakers for experiences that feel negative. Emotions like anger and blame usually come much later in life; as children, we tend to blame ourselves. Children don't have the emotional maturity to contextualize and understand the shortcomings and failures of their caretakers. Instead, because children see caretakers as their only source of safety and survival, they draw conclusions about themselves when needs aren't met or are met inconsistently. For example, because a child doesn't have the capacity to understand that mom is trying the Ferber Method (cry it out) because it was trendy in the 80's, and that's the reason she isn't coming to when when they cry, nor that mom is doing the best she can with the resources she has at the moment, the child will naturally look for self-adjustments to make in order to try and have their needs met. Repeated on a larger scale, a child may draw an internal conclusion that their voice doesn't matter, or that vocalizing distress results in a negative outcome. When that child is an adult, she may have difficulty voicing dissent or communicating her needs to her partners.

    Obviously this is a wildly simplified example, but once you understand the mechanism, you can then understand that you, as a child, didn't have the internal resources to understand the reality of your caretakers' behaviors. That very important realization can help you begin to explore what conclusions you may have drawn as a child based on your perception of your caretakers' behaviors and your interactions with them. I will also reiterate here that your caretaker's did not have to be overtly harmful, abusive, or have mal-intent to cause a child to draw harmful or untrue conclusions. It is our perception at that moment and the resulting emotions that drive the beliefs and behaviors we carry into adulthood. Clients will often say to me that their parents are loving and supportive and that their childhood was genuinely good. That can be entirely true and that same client may have still drawn a conclusion or developed a belief about themselves or about love that is harmful or just not true. We don't have to assign blame to cultivate the self-awareness necessary to understand where the foundations of our maladaptive behaviors came from.

 Essentially, there's no way around drawing conclusions as a child; our brains are designed to work this way. As an interesting and relevant example of this, there is a particular part of the brain that I often talk about in my work with clients that is designed to predict and recognize rejection, as well as urge us to recalibrate whenever it senses rejection in order to earn acceptance. In our evolutionary history, this helped our ancestors survive.

 Think about it— in a society where you would absolutely need your tribe in order to eat, stay warm, stay safe, and navigate the wilderness, your brain's ability to sense rejection and internally motivate you to change in order to ensure you can re-gain acceptance would be a pretty useful skill. This skillset is especially active when we're children and in the process of learning who we are, where we stand in the world and in relation to others around us, and how to have our needs met in the most reliable way possible.

For me, experiences that felt invalidating from the people that were most important to my survival translated to a core belief that I wasn't important; essentially a belief that I wasn't enough. I learned that there was something wrong with me, but– remember that internal drive to recalibrate to ensure acceptance?– my developing brain came up with ways to meet the need for validation. The rejection I perceived triggered my brain to create a coping skill to compensate.

Growing up, it manifested as perfectionism. I wanted validation from my caretakers, and I figured out that the best way to get it was through good grades, good behavior, and all the effort I could muster to be the kid I believed my parents wanted me to be.

The older I got, the more my desire for validation expanded beyond my caretakers and to anyone who could help me fill the need I had. It was a pattern I recognized in myself when I began my own healing journey– and a pattern I could definitely see in my dating history when I took the time to look. And the most important thing I realized? I couldn't really allow myself to love or be genuinely loved as long as I was holding onto the belief that I was lacking in some way, or the belief that I needed validation from anyone other than myself.

Jenna came to me after ending a 15 week relationship with a guy she thought could have been the one. The thing was, she had a long history of not-long-but-not-that-short connections that she was struggling to understand. She had been single for years, and kept ending up in what she referred to as "mini-relationships" with men who ended up being way more dysfunctional than she thought at the beginning.

"Things are going great and I really think the relationship will finally end up somewhere, and then I discover they're... let's see, hoarder-level filthy, emotionally unavailable, drowning in debt and not willing to fix it, an alcoholic, still hung up on their ex, and total mommy's boy, oh, and one cocaine addict, but 'only on the weekends.' she ticked off three years of relationship death blows.

I asked Jenna to explore what happened in the beginning of those relationships. I wanted to know what was happening to make her overlook what red flags warning signs there were to end up with so many men who were so ill-suited for her. We needed to identify how she was choosing the men that she was choosing and why it was taking her so long to discover their fatal flaws.

We were only about half way through this first session when I realized that Jenna knew these men had issues, long before the relationships would end. She explained that she didn't always realize the extent of their issues, and she certainly wasn't choosing them on purpose, but in all cases, she really liked each of the men she had dated. When she discovered their own lives weren't 100% together, she believed they had enough potential to be really amazing partners. They just needed the right circumstances, the right support.

"So, they just need *you*?" I prompted.

Jenna paused. "I– well, I suppose. I bring a lot to the table, it's not surprising that I have the resources and ability to help people I care about. I *want* to help the people I care about, that's part of being a good person and a good partner."

Jenna wasn't wrong. She did bring a lot to the table. She was beautiful, successful, put together, and obviously going places. She had an amazing job that she excelled at and resources to spare. In addition to being high achieving, she was big hearted and kind, and I didn't have any problem believing that she did genuinely want to help people. In this case, however, she was helping to her own detriment.

I asked Jenna where she felt the best in her life– what area of her life she felt like things were the most "right." Without hesitation, she replied, "Oh, I love my job."

She explained that not only did she enjoy her work, but she was good at it. She loved feeling capable and accomplished. She loved feeling respected and the feeling that she was putting all of the pieces of the puzzle into place in a way that only she could. As we explored how being good at her work made her feel, I also asked her to think about when she didn't feel that way, aside from in her recent relationships.

"I always felt successful at work— work and school have always come easily to me. Some of my favorite memories are the ones where I've really succeeded in what I was doing, winning awards, being recognized, that kind of stuff. But growing up, I felt like my social standing didn't reflect that version of myself. I didn't have a lot of friends— I wasn't popular. I was a little heavier as a kid. You know, just chubby and awkward in the way that smart kids sometimes are."

Jenna went on to describe her upbringing with immigrant parents who had worked hard, but struggled. They pushed for and rewarded success. Her dad struggled with anxiety and often self-medicated with alcohol— her mother overlooked any poor behavior on his part citing how hard he worked as a reason for any coping methods he engaged in. Jenna admitted she grew up believing that achievement and conventional success would solve all of this. Specifically, her eventual success would solve all of the problems her family had faced.

I gently suggested to Jenna that she was repeating the same family pattern with her romantic partners. Her belief that she had to be successful and that her success could save her family and solve all problems had translated into a grown-up belief that she was capable of saving or fixing any potential partner she ended up with through the power of her own success.

She was excusing bad behavior, misaligned values, and underachieving partners with a belief that her own accomplishments and achievement would raise them up.

We explored how success had been the frame through which she experienced validation, connection, and love as a child and as an adolescent. Success was her love-substitute. Jenna wasn't dating looking for a compatible, healthy partner; she was dating looking for a project she could succeed at. At the depth of her being, Janna wanted love; but she was settling for any avenue she could find that would allow her to show she was good enough and prove her worth.

Jenna would continue to struggle with choosing partners until she embodied her worth *outside of her success* and got comfortable with receiving love from a person that she couldn't help or fix. We spent the rest of our time together cultivating Jenna's sense of self worth, developing internal boundaries in which Jenna learned to stay on her side of the street in her relationships (all of her relationships, not just romantic ones!), and helping her recognize when she was using chasing success as a love substitute.

    Jenna did vastly improve the men she was picking in her dating process and the amount of time she was willing to tolerate the types of men who were really just projects. A little more than six months later, she met an architect who didn't need fixing. In fact, he didn't need Jenna for anything other than building an amazing relationship. She had successfully pivoted from her love-substitute to the real thing.

    I don't say that lightly– I know it isn't an on / off switch. And I also know that there are still days when Jenna struggled with the fact that her architect didn't need her for anything– the part of her that had relied on her love-substitute for so long was triggered. For me, there are still days when that little girl who didn't believe she was important crops up. I am by no means "fixed", and I do not believe that you need to be "fixed" to find love. What I do believe is that you have to be in a place where you are willing and able to look at your unmet needs, childhood wounds, and all of those tactics you've developed to try and meet them in order to begin the journey of learning the true source of all of the love, validation, attention, an acceptance you've been searching for– you.

Walking that pathway is probably a lifetime journey– you'll be the first to know if I ever reach the end. It's when we try to pretend the problem and the pathway don't exist, drowning our deeply hidden sorrows in our own personal love-substitutes, that we block ourselves from the real deal.

CREATING BETTER LOVE:
THE ROOT OF YOUR LOVE SUBSTITUTES

The place to begin exploring your own love substitutes lies in their roots. It is ultimately both empowering and impactful to understand not only what our love substitutes are, but to understand where they came from in the first place. Use the following prompts to begin your own exploration and reflection.

Our goals in this process are:

1. To consider our own love substitutes as they've shown up in our adult life and explore where they may have come from in our past.

2. To familiarize ourselves with our own beliefs around our worthiness and lovability, and begin to dismantle the version of ourselves we believed we had to be in order to deserve love.

Consider the following prompts. As always, resist any urge to edit or soften the responses that come to mind for you. Honesty will make this exercise more impactful.

1. Consider your childhood and adolescence. Did you believe that you were inherently worthy of love, support and validation? Did you openly and freely receive those things from your primary caretakers and/or family of origin? If not, what became the easiest, most available way for you to experience those feelings for yourself?

2. What did you need the most from one or both of your primary caretakers that you didn't receive? How have you tried to meet that need as an adult?

3. What did you have to do or who did you have to be in order to receive love, validation, or support from your primary caretakers or family of origin? How is that version of you similar or different from how you have shown up in your adult relationships?

– CHAPTER ELEVEN –
TIGHT PANTS AREN'T ALWAYS THE ANSWER

There comes a time in every woman's life when her well-meaning friend will insist on setting her up, because *"what's-his-face is just oh-so-perfect for you and oh my god you two will just hit it off and I can't believe I didn't think of it before you'll just looove him!"* Objectively, I can't say this is always a terrible idea, mostly because absolute statements are difficult to defend, but from personal experience, it has not worked in my favor.

But, before we move on with my story, I do want to remind you that it is a very good dating practice to let the people in your life know that you're looking for a relationship and open to being set up, open to being invited to events where you might meet someone special, and otherwise open to support from the people around you who know you best. Set ups and blind dates are not always winners, but the potential is always there, and most of us could use a little dating practice now and again. Always be safe meeting people you don't know, whether from a set up or an app, and opt for public places where you feel comfortable. But by all means, be open!

Moving on...

Kristen, childhood friend extraordinaire, set me up the summer after senior year. I didn't really date in high school, and she decided that she could help me break the ice– the rest would fall into place. Unbeknownst to me, she had set her sights on Andrew, a tall, Italian guy who drove an '89 Mustang and listened nearly exclusively to the Rolling Stones. Also unbeknownst to me, he had just been dumped by his former, very serious, very long-time girlfriend– named Carrie.

You don't know awkwardness until you've experienced looks of shock, horror, and polite cover-up smiles on each person's face as your new boyfriend makes introductions.

When it came time for the actual going-on-a-date part (thanks to Kristen), I struggled a bit with how to dress. Actually, I was clueless. I had never been on an actual date before, and my inner critic was running at top speed. When I called Kristen to ask, her response was, "Anything but what you normally wear."

In the fall following that summer, I would be heading to art school. Even though I hadn't left for school yet, I had totally embraced the role of unkempt art student. My general uniform consisted of baggy jeans– always a size or two larger than what I actually wore– and thrifted classic band t-shirts. Accessories consisted of paint splatters from the latest painting I had been up all night working on, and old, beat up converse, but only when I had to.

After seeing my wardrobe and having labeled me as hopeless, Kristen insisted on a shopping trip, and, at her insistence, I ended up in the tightest jeans I had ever owned and a blue top with what can only be described as a plunging neckline. I looked nothing like myself, and I felt 100% uncomfortable.

I took her, and my other friends' advice on how to act on the date, what to talk about, and how to do my makeup and hair. I grilled my parents about what they thought about him, what they knew about his family, and how I could impress him. Everytime he called or texted, I panicked a little and asked the people around me how I should interpret the message and how I should respond.

Because I felt inexperienced and not good enough, I assumed that being anything but myself was probably the best way to go. I chose to let the people around me dictate who I presented myself to be with Andrew. And I was very concerned about whether he would really like me or not.

From an outside perspective the date was … fine. Genuinely, fine. Nothing more, nothing less. There was nothing remarkably terrible or remarkably amazing about the date itself; but to this day, I'm not sure I've ever been more uncomfortable. I was uncomfortable in my clothes, uncomfortable in my skin, and spent most of the date trying to remember the advice I had collected rather than enjoying the actual time I spent with the guy I wanted to like me so much.

I talk a lot about authenticity in this book—there's an entire chapter dedicated to leading with authenticity in every aspect of dating, from your dating profile and who you connect with to communicating your needs and desires to those you connect with. I'm sharing the story of my tragically boring first date because I've learned that an outward measure of authenticity requires an internal commitment to yourself that makes being authentic with others possible.

It wasn't possible for me to show up as my authentic self on my date with Andrew— sure, in part because I was genuinely nervous and it truly was my first date ever, but also because I lacked a true sense of who I really was. I let everyone around me tell me who I should be in an attempt to gain approval from a boy I liked. But that didn't start with my first date or with Andrew; it started when I was much younger.

You'll learn in this book, if you haven't already, that basically everything starts when we're much younger.

I would learn in my own healing journey that many of my relationship struggles were linked to core wounds that I had experienced as a child. When I understood the nature of my wounds, it became a lot easier to understand why I struggled to be my authentic self on my first date, and on many dates after. And why I then ended up in relationships that had no space or tolerance for who I truly was.

Core childhood wounds impact our adult relationships because they're rooted in developmental trauma– they impact the way we interpret what it means to successfully be a human in relationship to other humans and surviving the world we live in. They're always designed to keep us safe and to attempt to ensure the people around us are meeting as many of our emotional and physical needs as possible, but they rarely result in an accurate understanding of how sustainable, healthy, fulfilling relationships are formed and maintained.

Core wounds can usually be classified in one of five categories:

Abandonment Wounds:

People living with an abandonment wound experienced physical or emotional abandonment from a primary caretaker or person of significance in their childhood. These individuals often fear abandonment in their adult relationships, don't like being alone, and usually display patterns of codependency, in which they sacrifice their own needs and wellbeing for another person, in order to ensure the other won't leave them. They may be plagued by a feeling that they don't matter or aren't important. Those with abandonment wounds may have a history of attracting emotionally unavailable partners or partners who avoid commitment and future planning.

Abandonment wounds can be caused by the physical abandonment or absence of a parent or primary caretaker, but can also be caused by the emotional experience of abandonment. Emotional abandonment is characterized by being disregarded, devalued, or dismissed by primary caretakers or a person of significance. Examples of emotional abandonment might include a parent/caretaker with an illness or addiction who is unable to be emotionally present, the use of the silent treatment or being ignored as a form of punishment, or even consistently being sent to your room to be alone in moments of high emotional need.

Betrayal Wounds:

Betrayal wounds occur when a child is betrayed by a primary caretaker or person of significance and is still faced with depending on that person for his or her needs to be met. These individuals value control in their relationships and prefer not to have to depend on another person for anything. They usually have difficulty trusting people, and also struggle to trust themselves, especially when it comes to discerning the intentions and motivations of others. They often do not feel safe in relationships and may even have resigned themselves to the belief that betrayal is bound to happen in their relationships no matter what they do.

Those living with betrayal wounds tend to attract partners who fulfill their subconscious belief that betrayal is inevitable and partners who allow them to be in control as often as possible. Betrayal wounds can also lead to betrayal blindness, in which a person may have the tendency to minimize or ignore the betrayals of the people they are in relationship with, and as a result, will stay stuck in relationships despite a pattern of betrayal from another person. Betrayal in childhood can look like physical or emotional abuse, the parent witnessing the abuse not stepping in to protect the child being abused or disregarding the child's cries for help, a caregiver or person of significance consistently breaking promises or not keeping their word, or a persistent experience of dishonesty from caretakers or a person of significance.

Injustice Wounds:

Injustice wounds occur when a child has significant and persistent experiences that feel unfair, usually at the hands of rigid, emotionally distant caregivers who have high expectations and leave little room for error or learning. Their childhood experience is marked by learning that performing well is more important than honoring one's feelings or experience. As a result, those with injustice wounds never learned to connect with their caregivers with any emotional depth or vulnerability and are often cut off from their own emotional experience as an adult.

As an adult, the person with injustice wounds will hold both themselves and others to often impossibly high standards, striving for perfection. They have difficulty accepting criticism and hesitate to accept help or rely on others for support. Those living with injustice wounds are not usually in touch with their emotions and do not show vulnerability to others, all while continuing to over-value performance and perfection Injustice wounds make intimacy in relationships difficult, and those living with injustice wounds may struggle to form close relationships, use fault-finding as a protective mechanism to keep other people at arm's length, struggle to say no, and experience anger and resentment often. They tend to attract relationships with people they can save or fix.

Neglect Wounds:

Neglect wounds occur when a child experiences persistent neglect of his or her physical, emotional, or psychological needs. Neglect wounds can show up in adult relationships as a sense of disconnection or emptiness, low self esteem, a heightened sensitivity to rejection, confusion about the expectations of others or even one's own expectations of self. As adults, those with neglect wounds will often have difficulty identifying needs and ensuring that they are met, sometimes with a pervasive feeling that he or she may not deserve to have their needs met. Adults carrying neglect wounds may unconsciously choose partners who are emotionally unavailable or incapable of meeting their needs, as they often have an underlying belief that their needs aren't important. Neglect wounds can also result in an overall resistance to intimacy and closeness.

Humiliation Wounds:

Humiliation wounds occur in children who are belittled, degraded, or made to feel shame (remember, shame is the feeling that something is wrong with who you are, as opposed to guilt which comes from a feeling that something you did was wrong). As a child, the person with humiliation wounds likely had persistent experiences that caused them to believe their caretakers were ashamed of them or their behavior. This person often feels sorry or bad as an adult, and may help others to the degree of over-giving or self-abandonment as a subconscious way of trying to be good enough or compensate for the shame they felt as a child. At the same time, they will neglect their own needs and desires and may experience feelings of guilt if they focus on themselves.

In relationships, the person with humiliation wounds will struggle to receive from their partner, often not feel good enough, and either choose partners who are underfunctioning and leave a lot of space for them to give and care-take, or they will choose partners who affirm the way they already feel about themselves, in other words, partners who criticize, belittle, or humiliate them. Humiliation from a partner might look like flirting with other people in public, infidelity, veiled or outward criticism in front of other people, or jokes at their expense, for example.

You may find that you relate to more than one of these core wounds. Whether there's one that stands out or you can see parts of yourself in several of the descriptions, all of these core childhood wounds stemmed from childhood experiences that likely taught you to create a false version of yourself in order to survive, navigate, and find a place in your family of origin or the home you grew up in. In order to cope with the reality of your experiences and try to have as many of your needs met as possible, there were parts of yourself you learned to suppress or disconnect from, leaving them underdeveloped.

In turn, you most likely also learned to overdevelop other parts of yourself as a way of coping with the pattern of unmet needs you experienced as a child.

And when we spend our developmental years acting out a false version of ourselves and our childhood wounds go unhealed, we will almost always perpetuate our false selves in our future, adult relationships. We learned that was the version of us required to be safe, be accepted, and be loved. That means we're not only going to show up as out false selves in our relationships, but we'll also be subconsciously attracted to people and relationships that allow us to show up as that false version of ourselves, both because it's familiar to us and because part of us believes that we have to be that version of ourselves to experience love. Choosing relationships that reflect that belief make our subconscious mind feel like we're more likely to be loved and accepted, and relationships that fall outside of that belief will feel uncomfortable and triggering, even if they're good.

My primary core wounds are abandonment and humiliation wounds, and as a result I struggled with feelings that I wasn't good enough, shame, and a fear of not being wanted. Those wounds left me constantly unsure of myself and of how others felt about me— I anticipated rejection and always felt like I had to look outside of myself for assurance. In retrospect, my first date encounter wasn't surprising at all. I assumed others would know what I needed to do and be in order to be accepted by my date because my childhood experiences had taught me that I wasn't able to be sure of myself and who I truly was didn't matter.

The false version of myself was carefully curated and relied entirely on other people's input to tell me what was acceptable and what wasn't. I brought nothing to the table on that first date with Andrew— I was too busy being everything everyone else told me to be and waiting for cues from my date that he was in approval.

I was too worried about whether Andrew liked me to ever pause and ask myself if I even liked him. My false self treated dating like an ongoing audition, but I was the only one trying out. The truth was, I wasn't dating to find compatibility, I was dating to find approval.

If you want to improve your relationships, you have to start being curious about what version of yourself is showing up in your connections. You have to be willing to explore the parts of yourself that you may have suppressed long ago. And you must be willing to engage in a process of discovering and nurturing your most authentic self.

When Lola came to her first appointment with me, she was newly back on the dating scene and frustrated. She described a string of short-lived connections that seemed promising, until each guy would ghost her after a handful of dates. The end of each potential connection left her feeling worse about herself than the one before. On our call, she hypothesized that she had been out of dating for too long, wasn't the 'type' of girl guys these days were interested in, and that the apps were out to get her.

I asked Lola to describe to me the type of person she was looking to create a relationship with and the process she was using to choose the men she continued to see.

She paused before listing a collection of mostly non-descript terms that could have described half of the men in New York City. "Tall, good looking, has a job and his own place, wants to get married and have kids one day..."

When it came to her selection process, she was even less detailed. "I'm not sure, I just look for a vibe– like good chemistry. And if we both want to see each other again, I like to give things a real chance, because you never know, right?"

I asked Lola if there were ever men she decided she didn't want to give a chance to, even if they were interested in her, to which she said, "No, not really any that I can think of."

I tasked Lola with creating a more specific framework for the hypothetical person she believed would be an ideal match for her, and I encouraged her to think about the version of herself that was showing up on the dates she was accepting (a.k.a. all of the dates offered).

We explored how she felt when she was on a date, how she spoke and acted with the men who asked her out, and what it would feel like for her to turn them down. She immediately got emotional. "I don't know why, but it feels like I can't say no. If they're interested in me, it's like

I'm automatically interested back. And once I know they want me, I can't stand the thought of being rejected by them. I never end up realizing that I didn't like them that much until after they're long gone."

I asked Lola who else had made her feel that way in her life. She shrugged, "I always felt rejected by my grandfather. He and my grandmother took care of me and my siblings after my dad left, and he never really seemed like he wanted us there."

She explained that she did whatever she could to help her grandmother and keep her younger siblings from bothering her grandfather, who always seemed to be in a bad mood no matter what she did. Her happiest moments were when her dad would visit, but the visits always felt too short.

As we worked together through her childhood experience, Lola started to realize that she was treating acceptance from the men she was dating the same way she treated the visits from her dad when she was young– she took whatever she could get, and she was grateful for it.

It wasn't surprising that she hadn't learned to treat dating as a process of selecting a good match, nor that she attracted emotionally unavailable men who didn't want to commit. Her abandonment wounds were essentially running her adult dating experience. Because she learned as a child to take what acceptance and attention she could get from her dad, all while molding herself into the version of herself she thought might receive a little less rejection from her grandfather.

That was the version of herself choosing the men she was dating and showing up on her dates. Her six year old self was running her love life, and she was auditioning for men hoping they would choose her without ever giving her authentic self a real say. Every time a man chose her for a date, her inner child felt like dad was choosing her all over again. And she had to do anything she could not to mess it up.

Lola and I worked over several weeks to reconnect her with her inner child and the parts of herself she had suppressed as a result of her childhood wounds, namely, the part of herself that had preferences and desires that were worthy of acknowledgement. Lola realized that she wouldn't be able to shift the reality of her dating life until she healed the part of herself that had been auditioning for love and acceptance for the last twenty years.

As Lola practiced dating from a place of honoring her desires and using dating as a tool to find a genuine match, she had to learn to self-soothe the anxiety that would come up around ending connections and telling people no, but now that she could see the pattern, it was almost impossible to ignore. Understanding how her childhood wounds were dictating how she showed up in her relationships gave Lola the insight she needed to develop new strategies for soothing her inner child and learning to date as her most authentic self.

Being more selective and saying not to the men who didn't meet her newly-realized standards definitely meant that Lola had less dates. She definitely complained in a few of her sessions with me that she felt like there were less options available to her. But you don't need more people to be successful at dating; you need the right people, and eventually the right person.

Several months later, Lola did find the right person. As of this writing, they've been together for nearly two years.

As for myself, Andrew and I had a few more mediocre dates, but the relationship really couldn't go anywhere. It would take me years to recognize my own wounds and how they were impacting my ability to be myself. I kept hoping that the right relationship with the right person would show up and make me feel safe enough to be who I was. I had to learn that being my most authentic self was what would empower me to find the right relationship with the right person.

The questions at the end of this chapter will help you begin to explore your own wounds and where they may be showing up in your dating life and your adult relationships. Be gentle and kind with yourself as you work through them. The best place to start is compassion for yourself and your inner child.

CREATING BETTER LOVE: CORE WOUNDS

Exploring our core wounds can be a challenging and vulnerable experience. Engage in this process with compassion, gentleness, and with the support of a professional if you feel that is necessary for your safety and wellness. Please also remember that having or identifying with any of the types of core wounds explored in this chapter does not require that you had a "bad enough" or "traumatic enough" childhood. Many of my clients will hesitate to even explore the concept of core wounds because they didn't have an abusive, angry, or obviously traumatic childhood. Remember that trauma is subjective—there is no "bad enough" scale. Rather, it is any experience that dysregulates your nervous system; any experience that is dramatic, isolating, unexpected, or leaves you with no strategy as to how to move forward.

Our goals in this process are to:

1. Explore our own core wounds with compassion and kindness toward ourselves.

2. Gain an understanding of our own developmental experience and how it has impacted our current relational

reality.

3. Begin to develop strategies to address and heal our core wounds without allowing them to continue to unconsciously play out in our relationships.

As you explore the following prompts, be sure to take your time and seek out professional support as needed. Release any expectations that you have to heal these wounds immediately– time and grace are far more essential to healing than strict timelines ever will be.

1. As you read this chapter, which descriptions, if any, of the types of core wounds resonated with you? Which parts did you most relate to?

2. Find a picture of yourself as a child, if possible, or simply practice imagining your younger self. Practice asking your inner-child what he or she needs. What parts of their experience were ignored? What

emotions were minimized or ignored? Stay present with any emotions that come up as you connect with your younger self and commit to feeling them, even though you may not be used to doing so. Explore ways to give your inner-child more of what he/she needed then, now.

3. Brainstorm ways that you can practice self-validation. How can you be more mindful, encouraging, trusting of yourself, accepting of your limitations, or accepting of your feelings on a day-to-day basis? What would it feel like for you to live in a place of self-validation? What would it change for you?

– CHAPTER TWELVE –
YOU DESERVE MAGIC

Larry was not my first crush, but he was the first guy, from my perspective, to pay me any attention. I was a quiet, sensitive teenager with the tendency to overthink and over question everything. Larry was older than me, popular, with a seemingly endless stream of friends and people interested in him. He was charismatic, and knew how to make a girl feel like she was the only one in the room, and he often used that to his advantage.

I had no idea why he would ever be interested in me.

My parents, sensing a disturbance around their 4.0, scrabble-playing, church-going daughter, immediately forbid me from seeing him, in part because he was several years older than I was. Like the obedient child that I was, I listened, respectfully, and did not pursue a relationship with him, despite how insistent he was in his pursuit.

While I wasn't allowed to date him, I was able to go to prom with him. I'm not actually sure how I pulled this off, but before I knew it, I was getting ready in my bedroom with two of my closest girlfriends, and Larry was waiting upstairs with the type of flowers you wear on your wrist. As an aside, I never understood the wrist-wearing flower trend that goes hand in hand with prom— not then, and not now. Literally never, in almost any real-life situation will a guy show up at your door with hands-free floral accessories, but I accepted my floral bracelet with the giddiness that only belongs to senior prom.

He wore a white tux. I wore a black and white strapless gown, but, being uncomfortable with the size of my arms, as I was the size of just about everything on my body at that time, I insisted on also having a huge, rectangular strip of matching fabric as a shawl. Now - don't get me wrong, shawls and wraps can be cute. But even though this one came with the dress, it was not. The stiffness and largeness of the fabric made it impossible to drape gracefully around my shoulders. It didn't hang delicately. It didn't hang at all. Instead, it bunched up and over my shoulders, nearly to my jawline. I kept my arms bent, stiff and inflexible, struggling to hold it in place, but it insisted on rising ominously up and over my shoulders, rendering a sort of dracula-esque vibe, giving the illusion of a large, collared cape. It was not a good look.

To make matters worse, while having my hair done earlier that day, I had taken a picture of a girl with a loose, messy bun in the back, with little flowers woven throughout to the stylist. The image didn't show the front of the style, so I meekly asked the stylist just to keep the front simple. And, in her defense, she did - slicking my hair back into a tight, matronly bun. No bangs, nothing loose about it. While my round face and slightly chubby cheeks have gotten me carded well into my thirties, I have learned the power of a good fringe. So for me, this particular style was also not a good look.

My self-conscious meter was amped beyond any reasonable degree. I spent senior prom sitting at our table, too uncomfortable and scared to move, unsure of how to dance with a dracula's cape strangling my every move, and worried about how terrible my hair looked. My date, ever the social butterfly, spent the night making new friends, always coming back to the table to check on me before returning to the dance floor, each time leaving my hunched lower in my seat than the time before. I was working really hard to lose myself and my awkward bun in the sea of black fabric that surrounded me.

My senior prom and a night with the boy I desperately liked but wasn't allowed to date was passing me by, all because I didn't think my arms were small enough.

And, here's the thing– even though, at this point, nearly two decades have passed since prom night, I have fallen into a particularly human trap that so many of us do: *I sacrificed what could have been magic for my inner critic.*

You might be thinking – *"No way. I would never do that – just sit at a table during one of the highlight nights of senior year because of a weird shawl thing? No. Way."* But, listen, the magic I'm talking about has nothing to do with prom and everything to do with the magic the universe provides us day in and day out. And if you're being completely, perhaps shockingly honest with yourself, how many times have you opted out, not taken the leap, given up before you even started, missed the experience, watched from the sidelines, not stepped into your fully divine, inherent power because you were too busy criticizing yourself? How many times have you not shown up because your sneaky bitch inner critic convinced you that there was some imperfection worth waiting out?

Maybe you declined a spot in the photo because you'd really rather weigh 20lbs less or lose the baby weight before participating in any form of documentation that's going to last forever. Or, better yet, you disguise your own self-loathing by being "helpful" and offering to take the photo to avoid being a part of it. Perhaps you've avoided making that connection or taking that opportunity to speak because your inner critic has convinced you that you aren't good enough and no one would care anyway. *"Who are you that anyone would listen?"* that inner-bitch might ask, and you might be inclined to respond, "You're right. I'll just wait..."

Or, maybe you don't swipe on the people you're really interested in because you're too busy assuming they won't be into you.

Maybe you would never give your number to the cute guy in the produce section who is managing to somehow make avocados look really, really good because part of you is too afraid of what you believe is the impending rejection that would follow.

How many times have you canceled or declined a date because you let your inner critic convince you that you weren't good enough in some way, or that you should be more afraid of potential rejection than missing out on something potentially amazing?

Later that same night, I sat in Larry's car, windows fogged, still clutching my shawl, I wanted him to kiss me - really wanted him to kiss me. In retrospect, he was doing all the right, sweet things, but I was just too self conscious to meet him even a small percentage of the way. My inner critic raged on in my mind about rejection and embarrassment, and I listened. He took me home that night, without ever having made a move, and we kept in touch off and on after that.

Just a few years later, high school graduation barely behind us, I would get a call from my mom telling me that Larry had passed away. He tragically died waiting for treatment in an ER waiting room.

I never did get to kiss him. I never even told him how much I liked him.

I'm guessing at some point or another you've avoided stepping into something magical in the name of waiting for some earthly thing to look, feel, or be better. But the truth of the matter is, you are being presented with magical opportunities every day, begging you to step into the power and divinity with which you were created. And guess what? I can say with absolute confidence that God doesn't care about the size of your arms.

What actually matters is your magical, divinely created soul having a breathtakingly full human experience. *So leave your bulky shawl at your seat, and go dance, already.*

You will never have this day again, and the more you trust your divine spirit, the more your inner critic will shut the hell up. And the more you step into your power, focus on the experience, the moment, and being-ness of it all, the more you'll be pleasantly surprised at just how profoundly the universe shows up to meet you, time and time again.

I repeated this pattern time and time again after sacrificing my senior prom to my insecurities, though it wasn't always as big and as obvious. When I was deep into healing my relationship patterns and broken heart, I decided to start dating again. I created a profile, as one does, and I started connecting with men online, knowing full well that this part of my process would be about learning in practice.

I was definitely guilty of not pursuing people I was genuinely interested in because I assumed that they wouldn't be interested in me, but I caught that behavior early on in my healing journey. I realized that by not expressing interest in the people I was genuinely interested in, I was only sacrificing potential for the sake of my insecurities– just like I sacrificed my prom to an insecurity about my arms. It wasn't my responsibility to date by trying to predict other people's level of attraction to me– that was just my inner-self trying to avoid rejection by not taking any risks.

And then this particular pattern became blindingly clear when I met Ryan.

Ryan and I connected on a dating site after I had committed to reaching out to every person I was legitimately interested in– even the ones I thought were too hot, too cool, or too good for me. It was a practice in honoring the self worth I was learning to see.

Ryan was very hot, very cool, and my interest was piqued as soon as I saw his profile. I messaged him, as I had promised myself I would, but I honestly never expected to hear back. To my surprise, he messaged back. And after exchanging some banter via message, he asked to call. We had a great conversation and by the end, he had asked me out. We made plans to meet at a downtown bar. He was doing everything right.

But regardless of what he did or didn't do, I spent our entire short-lived relationship second guessing everything.

I panicked when he didn't text back fast enough, sure that it was because he wasn't really interested in me. I convinced myself that he was ghosting me, when he wasn't. And god forbid he had to cancel or reschedule plans; it was as if my internal self was so busy anticipating the rejection I thought I deserved from the guy I didn't think I deserved that I couldn't be present in the actual relationship. I spent the entire time we weren't together trying to figure out what I should do, say, or text to elicit some response from Ryan that would help me feel secure in the connection– something to prove he actually liked me.

When we were together, I enjoyed every bit of our time, but everything was tainted by an undercurrent of anxiety. It was like Ryan's security mixed with how perfect he seemed amped up my own insecurities. Emotionally, I wasn't prepared for that level of contrast with another person. In retrospect, I know I wasn't far enough along in my own healing journey to sustain a relationship with a guy like Ryan. It wasn't that Ryan wasn't great, or even that we couldn't have potentially had a great relationship. It was because I didn't believe I deserved a guy like Ryan. My own insecurities and my own anxiety, all of which were rooted in deeper issues of self worth, undermined my ability to see that potential as actually possible.

I slowly started to act out in response to my own internalized anxiety. I would distance myself in moments of trying to prove to myself I didn't care if Ryan liked me or not (I totally did). I would pick fights over trivial things, even non-existent things as a way of defending my fragile inner self. I was hunting for red flags where there were none to keep myself from feeling too much or being too vulnerable. All in all, I was sabotaging my good relationship to avoid rejection.

And I was successful.

Ryan and I broke up three months into our relationship. The breakup was mutual and unremarkable; we agreed that it wasn't working. But years later I would look back on that relationship with a lot of understanding and insight. I had so convinced myself that I didn't deserve a good relationship with a good guy like Ryan that I unconsciously made sure it would never work. Better to sabotage the relationship than be rejected.

Similarly, when I worked with Anna, her biggest frustration was that she kept attracting the same type of guy over and over and over. Her dating life and her relationship history was a seemingly unending loop of connections with the same type of person; like *Groundhog Day* with terrible partners. We started our work together in the usual place by talking about safety, our human tendency to recognize and recreate patterns, and so on.

It wasn't until after a couple of sessions of digging that we hit the emotional jackpot.

Anna had what she considered to be one successful relationship in her adult life. One person with whom she could remember feeling safe, accepted, seen, and good about who she was. And in this particular case, that level of acceptance and recognition felt like it made up for the dysfunctional, difficult, even borderline abusive parts of the relationship. In fact, she admitted in our appointment that she had spent most of her time with that partner rationalizing away his bad habits and bad behavior because he truly loved her for who she was.

On a hunch, I asked Anna to make a list of all of the partners she could remember who matched her same-guy-different-body pattern and then to honestly compare them to that one past partner in question- the one she felt accepted her unconditionally. To no one's surprise, they all had a lot in common, including their less-than-desirable traits.

I asked Anna if it was possible that she was choosing men, both consciously and subconsciously, who were similar to that one accepting partner because part of her believed that only a guy like him- a guy with addiction issues, communication issues, control issues, fidelity issues- would be able to truly accept her for who she was.

In tears, Anna nodded. She shared that she saw other people on the apps and in public who she logically could see were better suited to be partners, the kind of partner she thought she was looking for, but she didn't really believe that those kinds of men would be genuinely interested in her. She was keeping her own dating pool small and limited by choosing men who were flawed enough to be more likely to accept the flaws she perceived in herself. Anna was very elaborately avoiding the rejection she assumed would come if she pursued partners of a higher caliber.

She would never be able to expand that same-guy pattern if she didn't start with her own self worth issues and ultimately get comfy with the idea that some people would likely reject her along the way. But rejection is just feedback— it doesn't mean anything about who we are, what we're worth, or how much we deserve to be loved and valued for who we are. Rejection is a refinement of your choices.

If you're also trying to find love all while avoiding rejection, I have to tell you that I understand. And I also have to tell you that it won't work. Dating is full of rejection. In some ways, that's the entire point; saying no to the people that aren't a good fit for you, and allowing others to say no when you aren't a good fit for them. This is the primary mechanism for dating that will eventually lead you to finding the person who is right for you.

You cannot date and avoid rejection.

Holding onto that feeling of safety you think you're creating by not putting yourself out there is just like me clutching that shawl the night of my senior prom. You've sacrificed enough magic for your insecurities, don't you think?

See, the secret is that you are already worthy. The only reason that you might doubt what's truly available to you, the only reason you would make yourself smaller, and the only reason you wouldn't put yourself out there is because some part of you might not believe that you are already, entirely worthy.

Our only job is to be true to ourselves while trusting that magic is possible.

And love ourselves every step of the way.

– CHAPTER THIRTEEN –
THE TWO REQUIREMENTS: HAVE FUN & BELIEVE

Your next relationship, whether it be your soul mate or just the next step on your path to better love, isn't going to happen because that person breaks into your house while you binge Netflix and eat popcorn. If you're ready to date better and move forward on the path to finding an aligned partner, you must also put yourself into a position of actually meeting people and actually interacting with potential matches. It doesn't matter whether you're using an app, going out and chatting with potential matches organically, or any other manner of interacting with living, breathing human beings of the sex of your preference– each of those vehicles are neutral resources that will work the way you work them. Putting everything you've taken away from this book into action will require you to actually participate. Dating is a contact sport– you have to put yourself out there.

    When I initially began my journey to profoundly shift my relationships, I spent six months intentionally not dating. Taking breaks from the dating pool can be a powerful tool to help you reset and heal. At some point, however, when I was ready to move onto the next level of shifting my relationships by actually experiencing a relationship that was different, I had to wade back in. It can be tempting to get so caught up in the 'healing on my own' stage that we use it as an excuse to never put ourselves out there in ways that are vulnerable or scary. Many of my clients come to me stuck in this phase– they don't actually want to date, they just want to have a loving, forever partner– and maybe you relate. If that's the case, I hate to break it to you, but those loving, forever partners don't just appear out of thin air. Not only do you have to meet them in order for them to enter your life experience, but the process of dating is also an important part of preparing you for that next-level relationship.

Again, the vehicles and resources you choose to use to meet new people are entirely up to you, as long as whatever outlets you've chosen actually lead you to new people. When I was learning to put my own Better Love Rules into practice, I had valiantly decided that I was going to be bold and meet people the good old-fashioned way. I had visions of organically chatting with beautiful men on the train, smiling at strangers while I made my coffee at the convenience store in the morning, or striking up wildly interesting conversations with people on the street. Those visions and fantasies felt amazing, but I eventually had to come to grips with the fact that meeting new people that way was so wildly out of character for me it wasn't ever going to happen. Who was I kidding? I spent my train rides with my nose in a book, I walked to work with headphones in, and no one should be subjected to interacting with me *before* coffee in the morning. These realizations are what prompted me to try online dating for the first time.

Be encouraged! One of the beautiful things about dating is that you don't have to engage in the process in any way that doesn't work for you, as long as you're engaged in the process. You can meet potential partners on your commute to work, while you're in the store, or from the comfort of an app on your phone. There is no pressure to use any method of meeting that feels uncomfortable to you, as long as you're doing the work to meet people. That said, I will interject this one, single caveat: We've already established that dating is about growing and learning, and how you date is no exception. Be prepared to check your assumptions about how you meet people and how you date. When you begin to show up in new ways and date with a purpose, it isn't uncommon to also be surprised about the methods of dating that are available to you and how great they can be.

For example, many of my clients come to me with a chip in their shoulder around app-based dating. They assume it'll be terrible, that the people on certain apps are only interested in sex, that no one finds real relationships in that type of environment, and so on, but the vehicle you use for meeting people doesn't change the fact that the type of people and relationships you attract are ultimately a reflection of you, your relationship with yourself, and your beliefs. I encourage my clients to be open to experiencing new ways of meeting people, just like I did eventually have to learn to meet people organically and cultivate conversations with strangers on the street. You never know who you'll meet or how– one of my most lively stepping stone relationships happened because I struck up a conversation about types of lettuce with a guy in the produce department of my local grocer.

    When it comes to the women I work with around dating, especially those women who are ready to do it differently and date with the intention of finding love, I do make a few strong suggestions about how to engage in the dating process. In addition to actually being in the practice of meeting new people and, hopefully, dropping any assumptions you may be carrying around particular avenues or platforms designed to help you meet more people, I also encourage my clients to actually date. As in, I ask them to continually engage in the process of meeting and going on dates with people. Most women I work with on the modern dating scene don't actually date, they have small, serial relationships. They start out holding the intention of meeting new people and dating, but once they meet someone they are mildly interested in or who shows them interest, they tend to put everything else on hold and engage fully in that one interaction, with the hope that it's actually "the one." There are two big problems with this approach, both of which occur in your brain.

    The first is that when we begin to experience feelings of falling in love, our brains produce large quantities of dopamine and norepinephrine. These brain chemicals are responsible for those overwhelming feelings of excitement and hyper focus we're able to maintain early on in a relationship. Have you ever noticed how a new relationship leaves you feeling exhilarated? Or noticed how you're able to sustain dates that are hours long and remember everything your person of interest did and said (all to be re-hashed later over brunch with your girlfriends, of course)? And how the sexual chemistry can feel through the roof? Blame those two little brain chemicals, which, by the way, mimic the feeling of being on speed.

    The second problem is that at the same time your brain's levels of dopamine and norepinephrine are rising, levels of serotonin are dropping. They can drop low enough to resemble the levels found in people who have obsessive-compulsive disorder— which is exactly why we have the tendency to fantasize and obsess over new love connections. This process feels great at the moment, but it isn't so great for fostering reason, logic, and clear-headedness in the midst of our new connections. It creates a feeling of intimacy and connection that isn't yet real and isn't sustainable.

    To help women avoid this moth-to-flame trap, especially if they already know they tend to be susceptible to early-relationship patterns that just aren't working, I recommend they commit to dating no less than three people at once. Yes, you read that correctly— dating three people ensures that you are actually dating, and it also helps prevent you from over-investing in one single person or interaction before you've had time to thoroughly explore it. Finding, slowly getting to know, and dating three people requires time and energy— it forces you to divide your attention, divide your available time, and interact with your potential matches in a much more reasonable, measured way. Dating three people at once helps keep you moving on the dating path and gathering data about what you like and what you don't, without getting hung up on any one person prematurely.

    And when you do meet someone you would consider settling down with? You'll have a much better chance of knowing. And part of the way you'll know is that ending those other dating interactions won't be difficult.

    As you date, remember to have fun. Use your dating experiences as an opportunity to drop the negative self-talk and limiting beliefs you've been carrying around love, dating, and relationships and be open to finding something truly amazing. Enough with the internal scarcity dialogue— *I'm too old, I'm not pretty enough, there aren't any good men left, they only want sex*, etc. You are worthy of love and you deserve a good partner. You don't have to wait to be chosen anymore. You can find potential relationships that could be mind-blowingly right for you and have fun while you do it. Dating with a purpose, while an intentional process, isn't meant to be drudgery. You are allowed to enjoy yourself along the way– share meals, share stories, collect experiences, and just learn as much as you can about yourself and the world and love in the process. You have been designed for human interaction. Not every person you date will be your aligned match, but they are still human beings with their own inherent worth and value and the ability to connect on interesting and genuine levels.

And last, remember to give people a real chance. Don't get hung up on "your type" or any number of hyper-specific yet ultimately shallow attributes you may have decided along the way are deal breakers. If your previous standards worked, you likely wouldn't be reading this book. If there is any sense of connection and compatibility, give that person at least two or three dates to really unfold and demonstrate who they are. Don't worry about chemistry, chemistry can be cultivated and lasting relationships aren't built on chemistry alone. Love and dating researcher, Diana Kirschner, Ph.D. recommends evaluating new connections on a three part scale: 1. Is he genuinely interested in me? 2. Is he willing to grow? 3. Is he a good guy? She recommends being willing to continue to explore a connection with people who meet those criteria, even if they aren't your traditional type. As you continue to date, certain people will naturally fall off of your list or out of interest, and most likely, there will be new people that will take their place. Your job is to continue to date and to continue to look for replacements for the people who naturally fall off the list, and as you do, your selections will become more and more refined.

Even after you meet someone who you think might be "it", I recommend continuing to date for an additional month or two as you explore this potential relationship. As you do, the person you are considering a next-level commitment with should continue to open up to be more available and more willing to commit to you, and this should be demonstrated in words *and* behavior.. The interaction with this person should improve as time goes on and you should feel more and more able to be yourself with this person. When you're ready for a singular, committed interaction, you can stop dating and engage in the relationship you've chosen, but remember, the process is just as important as the destination.

– CHAPTER FOURTEEN –
SELF LOVE IS NON-NEGOTIABLE

The big, takeaway truth in this book is that creating better love begins and ends with you. There's a reason that these chapters aren't filled with tactics, ploys, and games to get a partner and keep them interested– you aren't meant to find love in a relationship, your relationship is meant to be a container for the love you and your partner are already learning to embody within yourselves. Self love is the catalyst for creating all of the better love you desire in your life. Self love sets your baseline standards for all of the interactions and relationships you encounter. Self love is your first responsibility– your relationships with others come second. If dating is the pathway, and the people you meet are the stepping-stones, then self love is the power and momentum that enables you to move forward in the process.

    The real reason your dating life feels like a disaster? It's not the type of people you attract, it isn't what you look like, how picky you are, or how witty or entertaining you are– your dating life feels like it isn't working because of all of the beliefs and self doubt simmering under the surface. Just like self love sets the foundation for all of your relationships, your lack of self love affects everything you do and every relationship you engage in. Better love requires us to break the habit of prioritizing our relationships with others over our relationship with ourselves. It is through self love that we break the illusion that everything we need isn't already contained within ourselves.

    It's at this point that most people look at me and shake their heads– "Yes! Let's do that!" they cry, images of insta-worthy bubble baths and spa treatments bouncing around in their heads. But, here's what we often get wrong about self love— it isn't just a one-and-done deal. Self love isn't an on-off switch; we cannot just decide to love ourselves and then go about business as usual expecting everything to be different. Self love has nothing to do with bubble baths, spa treatments, and mani-pedis, although those can be really great vehicles for showing yourself love. In actuality, self love is a process that requires commitment, practice, learning, unlearning, and growth. It takes time and effort to learn what it means to truly love ourselves and to unlearn the poor models of self love that most of us had growing up. We spend so much time and energy learning and being taught as children, and yet most of us are never taught the importance of or how to love ourselves. Our concept of self love is left to what we unconsciously absorb from our parents and caretakers, and trust me, those lessons in love aren't always great. Frankly, learning self love is a big reason you're here on this planet, living this life. The more you commit to learning to love yourself better, the more the relationships in your life will shift to reflect that, and the more you'll learn to recognize the relationships that aren't truly loving from miles away.

When Mark and I broke up, it was after a knock-down-drag-out fight after dinner one weekend. After a few hours of hashing out everything that was so clearly wrong with one another, we sat on opposite ends of the couch, both emotionally bruised, both exhausted. With a sigh, he told me he just wasn't into this anymore and asked me to leave. Twenty minutes later, I was standing outside of his building, clutching my things in the rain and wondering if I'd find a cab. It was not how I expected the evening to end, but, surprisingly, I wasn't angry.

I had grown so accustomed to needing his love and approval that my own feelings had taken a permanent back burner. Why? I wanted a happy ending. I wanted him to be the one, to fall madly and deeply in love and live happily ever after. I had come to associate his love and approval with a feeling that I was good enough. I felt worthy and secure when I was with him and in his good graces. But in reality, I had created an environment that was the furthest from secure as it possibly could be– I depended on him to feel loved. I had given him all of my power, thinking it was romantic.

Over the course of our relationship, I had come to accept his criticisms and passive-aggressive demands as truth. I worked hard to preempt his needs and be the person he seemed to want because people in love worked to make each other happy, right? Or so I told myself.

As I proceeded to walk back to my own apartment, I began to think. Obviously, the problem was that while I was working to make him happy, he couldn't have cared less about my happiness. Else why would I be soaking wet and lugging my things down the sidewalk? Or, I reasoned, perhaps I had done something wrong and triggered this whole, dramatic mess in some way (old habits die hard, as they say). In truth, he was a narcissist with some severe dysfunction of his own, but the entire relationship dynamic wasn't entirely his fault. I had set up yet another relationship where I placed a big, giant, impossible expectation on another person- in this case, my own happiness, fulfillment, and my entire experience of love.

It took me far longer than the twenty-block walk home to figure it out, but I had a pretty serious dysfunctional pattern of my own when it came to relationships. I was looking for another person to make me feel happy, fulfilled, and loved. I thought that's what the 'right' relationship would do for me. But in reality, I had made it impossible for any of my relationships to truly succeed, and my expectations were keeping me from attracting the types of partners I really wanted. I didn't come into my relationship with Mark with any foundation of self love. Instead, I expected that my relationships would bring the love into my life that I believed was missing.

Because I wasn't practicing any form of self love, any love that was offered to me seemed amazing. It's why I had a patterned history of ending up in relationships with people like Mark. It's why I spent my twenties simultaneously wondering if I was good enough and also sleeping with anyone who showed interest– I was trying to create the experience of being loved entirely through my interactions with other people. And when those relationships failed, it was so easy to blame the opposite gender, or Tinder, or online dating, or men in Philadelphia, or, or, or... but here's the hard truth for all of us: We are the common denominators in all of the relationships we're attracting. It's not *about* you as far as limitations or applying meaning to our relational experiences, but sometimes, it *is* you. The burden of doing the work to shift your relationships is yours, and it begins with self love.

Growing up, whenever my siblings and I visited a friend or family member, went to a party, or had dinner at another person's house, my mother always insisted we bring something— a dessert, flowers, or a bottle of wine. "Never show up empty handed," she used to say, to a chorus of sighs and eye rolls.

Now, I appreciate this advice more than ever, not only for the etiquette of visiting, but also for a foundation of healthy relationships.

There are few things more wonderful than sharing the experiences and joys of life with another person who totally gets it— gets *you*. Being on the same wavelength as another person and feeling completely and utterly comfortable in a relationship is more amazing than I can adequately describe in a single paragraph. But, that kind of joy and comfort is really difficult to come by if you're showing up to the relationship empty handed. Not only does it put an extreme amount of pressure on another person to completely fill your needs for love and happiness, but it's also a demand that's 100% impossible for anyone to meet.

A sense of self worth and an inherent sense of love can only come from you. We can learn and evolve and grow through our relationships with others, but the relationship of your dreams, whether you're dating and looking for the right person or desperately want to up level your existing relationship, can never come from two unfulfilled people somehow coming together with the expectation of the other making them whole. Relational wholeness HAS to come from two individuals committed to becoming whole, complete, and fulfilled in themselves who then come together to add to and enhance the beauty and love in their lives. Their love will compound one another's– as long as they aren't showing up empty handed. It all starts with committing to love yourself in real, tangible, profound ways.

So what is self love? The most important things to understand about self love are: It is a shift in mindset that prioritizes you showing up for the sake of your own dreams, feelings, and fulfillment. It is not a one-time decision, and it takes practice and learning. It is an ongoing, evolving process that grows with you and your needs as an individual. Here are a few of my favorite self love truths:

- Self love is choosing to prioritize yourself and making a commitment to doing the things that feel right, aligned, and best for you.
- Self love is a commitment to saying no to the things that don't feel right or don't support your dreams, growth, and goals.
- Self love is being kind to yourself, in actions and in words.
- Self love is choosing to surround yourself with people who support and encourage you to be the best version of yourself.
- Self love is taking the time to care for yourself, physically, emotionally, and mentally.
- Self love is making time to do things you value, make you feel good, or trying new things that you've always wanted to try.
- Self love is trusting your gut and making a commitment to yourself not to sway from

your convictions and desires just to please others.
- Self love is investing in yourself and your future.
- Self love is accepting yourself exactly where you are and choosing to believe that you have the ability to achieve anything you set your mind to.
- Self love is honoring your boundaries and your needs in relationships, even if you think it may upset someone else.
- Self love is a commitment to your growth, learning, and healing without the need for perfectionism.
- Self love is living in the expression of your full inherent worth and value.
- Self love is an expression of your divinity.

Your best relationship begins with *you*. When we commit to loving ourselves in profound, tangible ways, we stop relying on others– and our relationships– as our sole source of happiness, love, and fulfillment. It gives us permission to show up in authentic ways for our partners and ourselves, and to walk away when it isn't working. When we commit to loving ourselves, we can more authentically radiate positivity, happiness, peace, and confidence. We no longer have to doubt ourselves or second-guess our worth and value. Self love will raise your vibration and your standards and ultimately lead to amazing, beautiful possibilities that you may have never thought were available to you. And that level of self-generated attraction will start to attract equally as fulfilled and love-filled people.

    Choosing to love yourself will absolutely change your life, and will be the launching point for creating your best relationships. However, let me be clear about something– self love is not something you have to perfect or another impossible standard you have to live up to. I see you out there, reading this chapter, and wanting to turn the process of self love into something you can win or master, because I used to think the same thing. Self love is your natural state– it is a way of being and a way of moving through the world to which you have been divinely called. It isn't an impossible standard, and it certainly isn't that you won't attract a relationship until you've mastered it. We are all in the state of learning to love ourselves more and better–

whether you're actively dating or you've been married for 50 years. But your relationships will shift the more you engage in the learning process of self love. From a state of being immersed in self love, it becomes increasingly difficult to accept and participate in relationships that are out of alignment with who you are or that fail to honor your true worth and value.

So where does one even begin?

Start where you are. Perhaps you need to begin with self awareness– the act of just paying attention to our own needs, desires, and emotions can be absolutely revolutionary. Maybe your soul is calling out for self acceptance and a little less judgment or negative self talk. Maybe you need to learn to prioritize yourself. Wherever you are on the path to self love, know that you are always in the position of modeling for yourself and for others how you want to be treated and how you want your relationships to manifest in your life. The way you are learning to love yourself is the ground floor of the lessons and challenges we face in love and in the relationships in our lives. The state of your love life begins with you. Whenever you find yourself faced with the task of improving an existing relationship, breaking a stubborn pattern in your love life, or finding yourself faced with a bunch of lackluster dating options, turn your attention inward. Begin with an honest evaluation of where you are in your commitment to learning self love and the solution you're seeking won't be far behind.

You don't need to learn self love to prove your worth or make yourself worthy of receiving love. You're learning self love to remember that you were always worthy to begin with.

CREATING BETTER LOVE: SELF LOVE

If you leave this chapter with anything, I'd love for it to be a constant reminder that self love isn't something you get or you don't get— it's an ongoing, evolving process that you must commit to participating in. Each of us is already deeply and inherently worthy of love, but we don't always treat ourselves that way. In fact, most of us have a remarkable ability to put ourselves last and to move through life without ever considering what it means to truly show up and love ourselves. Use the following prompts to explore your beliefs and experiences about self love.

> Our goals in this process are:
> 1. To begin to explore our earliest experiences and models for self love and how they have impacted our own journey.
>
> 2. To recognize the places in our lives and relationships where we may not be showing ourselves the love we need.
>
> 3. To brainstorm new, inspired ideas about how we can better learn to show ourselves love.

Get out your journal and explore the following questions. Resist the urge to edit or second guess your answers. Whatever comes to mind is exactly what's intended to come up for you at this moment, and your journey toward self love can begin anywhere, even here.

1. Consider your primary caregivers as a child, whether they be your parents, grandparents, or someone else. What did they believe about self love? How did they love themselves? Since they likely didn't explicitly tell you, how did you know this?

2. How would you describe the examples that were set for you concerning self love while you were growing up?

3. If someone you cared about you were looking to you as an example of self love, what would they observe? What would they think you believed about self love based on how you live your life?

4. What would you need from yourself to feel more love? How could you care for yourself better?

5. Create your own definition of self love. What does it look like and feel

like to you? How would you know if you were loving yourself well?

As you consider the answers and insight that came to you while you explored the above prompts, begin to think about how you can redefine self love in your life right now. Consider practical, tangible ways you can begin to show yourself love and what things you could begin to do to love yourself better, starting today.

– CHAPTER FIFTEEN –
THERE ARE NO BAD DATES

Think of the guidelines in this book as gentle, but powerful mindset shifts that are intended to support you as you journey to become the whole, embodied, healed version of yourself– and are then empowered to call in whole, embodied, healed relationships. Depending on where you are in your personal journey, some chapters and insights may resonate more with you than others– take what you need right now, and know that as you continue to evolve, your perspectives will expand. You don't have to figure out how to date perfectly right now, tomorrow, or even next month– your job is to be willing to engage in your own personal process and allow your relationships and your dates to challenge you and grow you.

There are no bad dates. With few exceptions, every experience you have is worth having. Every experience you have holds potential value. Every experience you have is an opportunity to learn, even if it's to learn more about what you don't want in a relationship. There is meaning, learning, and gratitude to be found in every single date, both in the past and in the future. I want you to know that no matter how challenging your past experiences have been, no matter how many heartbreaks you've experienced, no matter how frustrated you are with your love life– you were made for this.

You were made for love, in all of its gorgeous, moving, soul-shaking forms, and romantic love isn't an exception.

In the midst of some of my most difficult moments, it was sometimes difficult to see the path in front of me. I struggled at times to keep the faith that I would actually meet someone worth settling down with and that my heart would ever be whole enough to experience a relationship that was light, happy, and forever. There were moments of anger, frustration, grief, and sadness. Learning the love lessons I had to learn in order to intentionally date and eventually create the relationship of my dreams sounds a lot easier in book form– actually living it is not linear and it can be challenging to keep the bigger picture in mind. Even when we lost sight of the path, our goals, or why we're even bothering– which is a very human thing to do from time to time– the path is always there. We can get back on any time, no shame, guilt, or self-flagellation required.

  Just over one year after I made the decision to learn to heal my relationship patterns, release my past, and date with conscious alignment always in mind, I found myself sitting in a tiny, Jersey diner on a Thursday waiting for my date to arrive. He was late, a detail I tease him about to this day, but once he arrived, coffee turned into drinks and drinks turned into hours of conversation in the parking lot long after everything had closed. That date turned into many, and within just a few months I knew this was the person I was going to marry.

And, I did.

Today, nearly a decade later, we are happily married and have been blessed with a beautiful home and beautiful children. He is everything I wanted and everything I need, even if I didn't realize it then. We are both still learning, still growing, and still evolving– together. And yes, because people always ask, my relationship does embody everything I included on my Love List, and then some. In fact, I still have the list I wrote back in 2010 before I met him! My relationship has provided me space to learn to become happier, more content, and more loved than I ever thought possible.

Here's why that's important for you– I'm not special. There is no secret or magic to calling in and creating the relationship of your dreams. It requires only that you show up with a willingness to experience, learn from, and have fun along your dating path. And, of course, it requires that you believe the relationship you're longing to create is possible. If there's any way to end this book, it is in this simple truth:

You, dear reader, hold within you the ability to create the love life of your dreams. Your desires and hopes when it comes to finding your match in another human being are intentional, purposeful, and yours to have. You are worthy of love, and nothing less than love that lights you up from the very depths of your soul. No matter what your past experiences have been in dating and in love, you are standing on the precipice of something truly different. You don't have to settle. You don't have to compromise. You don't have to be anything different than the awe-inspiring, intentional being that you are. Anything that makes you question the basic truth of your worth and value as a person is not love, and it is not meant for you. You don't need my permission or anyone else's to require more or to stand in the truth of who you really are, and the way you show up in your love life is no exception.

You've got this! I cannot wait to see the love you create in the world.

READY TO DIVE DEEPER?

You're in luck!

I know first hand how much of a learning and growing process embodying the guidelines of this book can be– and because of that, I created a free mini-course to help you continue your expansive journey. I've packed it with teachable moments, expanded commentary addressing some of the most common questions I get, and resources you can use to support the work that was included at the end of each chapter.

Sign up and access the course at no-cost at: www.KariTumminia.com/NBD-guide

ABOUT THE AUTHOR

Kari Tumminia is a love and dating coach, speaker, and author helping women from all over the world create better love by showing up as creative, empowered forces in their lives. Using over a decade of experience with powerful proven modalities, intuitive coaching, and some been-there-done-that tough love, Kari makes it possible for her clients to transform their love lives from the ground up- from refreshing perspectives on dating and improving existing relationships, to ultimately finding love within themselves to create relationships that are worth falling for.

Kari is an EFT (Emotional Freedom Techniques) expert. As a trainer and practitioner, she introduces her audiences to this accessible, life-changing self-care technique to conquer everything from first-date jitters to deeply held beliefs about love, worth, and value. She has been featured as a co-author and contributor for EFT Universe and Energy Psychology Press. This is her second book.

NO BAD DATES

Made in the USA
Middletown, DE
15 March 2022